The Alamo

Titles in the World History Series

WORLD HISTORY SERIES ■■■

DISCARDED

The Alamo

by
William W. Lace

18 1 8013

Lucent Books, P.O. Box 289011, San Diego, CA 92198-9011

J
F
390
L18
1998

Library of Congress Cataloging-in-Publication Data

Lace, William W.
    The Alamo / by William W. Lace.
        p. cm.—(World history series)
    Includes bibliographical references and index.
    Summary: An historical account of the first major battle in
North America between the cultures of the United States,
with its mainly British tradition, and that of Mexico, with its
history of Spanish rule.
    ISBN 1-56006-450-1 (alk. paper)
    1. Alamo (San Antonio, Tex.)—Siege, 1836—Juvenile
literature.   [1. Alamo (San Antonio, Tex.)—Siege, 1836.]
I.Title. II. Series.
F390.L18   1998
976.4'03—dc21   97–9863
                                                          CIP
                                                          AC

Copyright 1998 by Lucent Books, Inc., P.O. Box 289011,
San Diego, California 92198-9011

Printed in the U.S.A.

No part of this book may be reproduced or used in any other
form or by any other means, electrical, mechanical, or other-
wise, including, but not limited to, photocopy, recording, or
any information storage and retrieval system, without prior
written permission from the publisher.

Contents

Foreword

Each year on the first day of school, nearly every history teacher faces the task of explaining why his or her students should study history. One logical answer to this question is that exploring what happened in our past explains how the things we often take for granted—our customs, ideas, and institutions—came to be. As statesman and historian Winston Churchill put it, "Every nation or group of nations has its own tale to tell. Knowledge of the trials and struggles is necessary to all who would comprehend the problems, perils, challenges, and opportunities which confront us today." Thus, a study of history puts modern ideas and institutions in perspective. For example, though the founders of the United States were talented and creative thinkers, they clearly did not invent the concept of democracy. Instead, they adapted some democratic ideas that had originated in ancient Greece and with which the Romans, the British, and others had experimented. An exploration of these cultures, then, reveals their very real connection to us through institutions that continue to shape our daily lives.

Another reason often given for studying history is the idea that lessons exist in the past from which contemporary societies can benefit and learn. This idea, although controversial, has always been an intriguing one for historians. Those that agree that society can benefit from the past often quote philosopher George Santayana's famous statement, "Those who cannot remember the past are condemned to repeat it." Historians who ascribe to Santayana's philosophy believe that, for

example, studying the events that led up to the major world wars or other significant historical events would allow society to chart a different and more favorable course in the future.

Just as difficult as convincing students to realize the importance of studying history is the search for useful and interesting supplementary materials that present historical events in a context that can be easily understood. The volumes in Lucent Books' World History Series attempt to present a broad, balanced, and penetrating view of the march of history. Ancient Egypt's important wars and rulers, for example, are presented against the rich and colorful backdrop of Egyptian religious, social, and cultural developments. The series engages the reader by enhancing historical events with these cultural contexts. For example, in *Ancient Greece*, the text covers the role of women in that society. Slavery is discussed in *The Roman Empire*, as well as how slaves earned their freedom. The numerous and varied aspects of everyday life in these and other societies are explored in each volume of the series. Additionally, the series covers the major political, cultural, and philosophical ideas as the torch of civilization is passed from ancient Mesopotamia and Egypt, through Greece, Rome, Medieval Europe, and other world cultures, to the modern day.

The material in the series is formatted in a thorough, precise, and organized manner. Each volume offers the reader a comprehensive and clearly written overview of an important historical event or period. The topic under discussion is placed in a broad historical context. For example, *The Italian Renaissance* begins with a discussion of the High Middle Ages and the loss of central control that allowed certain Italian cities to develop artistically. The book ends by looking forward to the Reformation and interpreting the societal changes that grew out of the Renaissance. Thus, students are not only involved in an historical era, but also enveloped by the events leading up to that era and the events following it.

One important and unique feature in the World History Series is the primary and secondary source quotations that richly supplement each volume. These quotes are useful in a number of ways. First, they allow students access to sources they would not normally be exposed to because of the difficulty and obscurity of the original source. The quotations range from interesting anecdotes to farsighted cultural perspectives and are drawn from historical witnesses both past and present. Second, the quotes demonstrate how and where historians themselves derive their information on the past as they strive to reach a consensus on historical events. Lastly, all of the quotes are footnoted, familiarizing students with the citation process and allowing them to verify quotes and/or look up the original source if the quote piques their interest.

Finally, the books in the World History Series provide a detailed launching point for further research. Each book contains a bibliography specifically geared toward student research. A second, annotated bibliography introduces students to all the sources the author consulted when compiling the book. A chronology of important dates gives students an overview, at a glance, of the topic covered. Where applicable, a glossary of terms is included.

In short, the series is designed not only to acquaint readers with the basics of history, but also to make them aware that their lives are a part of an ongoing human saga. Perhaps they will then come to the same realization as famed historian Arnold Toynbee. In his monumental work, *A Study of History*, he wrote about becoming aware of history flowing through him in a mighty current, and of his own life "welling like a wave in the flow of this vast tide."

Important Dates in the History of the Alamo

1540–1542	1690	1718	1793	1803	1810	1819

1540–1542
Coronado's expedition travels through Texas

1690
First Spanish mission established by Franciscan friars

1718
San Antonio de Valero (the Alamo) established

1793
Last Spanish missions are withdrawn; Alamo is turned over to the military

1803
Louisiana purchased from France by United States

1810
Revolution begins in Mexico

1819
DeOnis Treaty cedes Florida to United States; United States gives up claims to Texas

1821
Stephen F. Austin allowed to start colony in Texas; Mexico becomes independent of Spain

1830
Decree of April 6 restricts North American immigration into and trade with Texas

1832
First skirmish between Texans and Mexico fought at Velasco

1833
Convention at San Felipe asks for creation of state of Texas; Austin is sent to Mexico City with petition

1834
Austin is imprisoned in Mexico City (January); Santa Anna removes Gomez Farias from office, becomes dictator (April)

1835
May: General Cós sent by Santa Anna to quell disturbances in Coahuila

June: Intercepted message at Anáhuac leads to surrender of Mexican garrison to Travis

July: Austin released from Mexico City

September: Austin, freed in July, reaches Texas and declares war; Cós lands with troops in Texas

October 2: First battle of Texas Revolution fought at Gonzales

October 5: Consultation at San Felipe proclaims Texas a separate state; Austin named to lead army

October 28: Battle of Concepción is fought near San Antonio; Austin leaves army; Santa Anna orders much of Mexican army to concentrate in northern Mexico

November 3: Consultation establishes provisional government for proposed state of Texas; Sam Houston named commander in chief of army

December 5: Battle of San Antonio begins

December 10: Cós surrenders San Antonio to Texans; Santa Anna begins march north

1836
January: Men and weapons taken from the Alamo for expedition to Matamoros; James Neill left in command

February 11: Neill relinquishes command of Alamo; James Bowie and William Travis agree to be co-commanders; David Crockett arrives at Alamo

February 12: James Fannin and troops arrive back in Goliad after deciding against Matamoros expedition

February 23: Mexican army enters San Antonio; Texans retreat to Alamo

February 24: Travis takes sole command, sends "Victory or Death" message; first Mexican artillery batteries placed

February 25: New batteries in place; La Villita burned

February 27: General Urrea defeats Matamoros expedition at San Patricio

February 28: Fannin begins march to San Antonio but returns to Goliad the next day

March 1: Thirty-two men from Gonzales arrive at Alamo; delegates arrive at Washington-on-the-Brazos for Constitutional Convention

March 2: Independence of Texas declared by Constitutional Convention

March 3: Bonham returns to Alamo with word that Fannin will not help; Travis draws famous "line in the sand"

March 4: Santa Anna calls meeting of officers to discuss strategy, decides to attack without waiting for heavy artillery

March 5: Santa Anna issues orders for attack the next day

March 6: Final assault on the Alamo begins at 5 A.M.; battle finished and all defenders killed by 6:30 A.M.

March 11: Houston arrives in Gonzales to take command of army

March 13: "Runaway Scrape," retreat of Houston's army and flight of civilians, begins

March 20: Fannin surrenders to Urrea after Battle of Coleto Creek

March 27: Fannin and troops are executed at Goliad

April 21: Santa Anna defeated by Houston at Battle of San Jacinto; Texas secures independence as separate republic

Viewpoints

The basic details of the Battle of the Alamo are simple. Slightly fewer than two hundred men, most North American, were trapped in an old church near San Antonio, Texas, by a Mexican army at least ten times their number. On March 6, 1836, after a siege of twelve days, the Alamo fell. All the defenders were killed. But why was the battle fought and what did it accomplish? It depends on one's point of view.

Soldiers in battle are often the least reliable sources of information. The roar of cannons, clashing of swords, shouts of encouragement, cries of pain—all under a thick blanket of smoke—make it unlikely that individuals can observe much more than whom they're trying to kill and who is trying to kill them. Except perhaps for the generals, directing troops from a safe distance, battles are seen from a very narrow point of view.

The viewpoints of the generals—indeed, of all survivors—can be just as narrow. Those who fight in battles can hardly be impersonal, impartial observers. They need to have been in the right, to feel that they have fought in a noble cause, perhaps to justify, both to others and to themselves, the slaughter that has taken place.

Historians, therefore, must be very careful when using the accounts of those who took part in historic events. What are their viewpoints? Are they using only some of the facts? Are they twisting others so as to give themselves credit or avoid blame? And what about those who did not take part but who write about such events? Do their causes or political fortunes stand to gain or lose depending on whether people believe them? One writer's terrorist may be another's freedom fighter.

The Battle of the Alamo is a good example of how viewpoints can differ. Those inside the walls thought they were upholding the cause of liberty against a tyrant. Those outside thought they were putting down an armed rebellion by their own citizens and fighting off an invasion by a foreign power. Both, to an extent, were correct.

A Battle of Cultures

Viewpoints on the Battle of the Alamo differ so widely—then and now—because it was more than a battle between soldiers. It was the first major battle in North America between the cultures of the United States, with its mainly British tradition, and that of Mexico, with its history of Spanish rule. While both sides saw the Texas Revolution as a fight for freedom,

The Mexican army charges the Alamo—engaging in the first major confrontation between the cultures of Mexico and the United States.

the underlying cause, writes historian T. R. Fehrenbach, "was extreme ethnic difference between two sets of men, neither of whom, because of different ideas of government, religion, and society, had any respect for the other."[1]

Perhaps because of this lack of respect, the Battle of the Alamo quickly became a legend. Newspapers and journals in the United States, in the months after the battle, portrayed the defenders as gallant American heroes, facing overwhelming odds, who gave their lives for liberty against the cruel dictator of an inferior nation. And since the rebels eventually won the war and Texas later became a part

of the United States, this viewpoint has been handed down over the years in American textbooks, fiction, and motion pictures. History, it is sometimes said, is written by the winners.

To get at the truth concerning the Battle of the Alamo, one must go beyond the legends—Jim Bowie and his famous knife, Davy Crockett with coonskin cap and rifle Old Betsy, William Travis drawing a line in the sand. All the viewpoints must be examined, fiction separated from fact. A basic question then remains to be answered: After all that has been written and sung about the Battle of the Alamo, what was its real importance to history?

1 The Mission

Despite the famous battle fought there, the Alamo was a church, not a fort. For seventy-five years after its founding in 1718, it was used by Spain in an attempt to convert the Indians of Texas to Christianity. Only later was it used to hold off an army. In the end, it had little success either way.

Spain never seemed to know quite what to do with Texas, and much of the time did not seem to care. Vast as it was, the land north of the Rio Grande (river) was a small and unimportant part of Spain's holdings in the New World. The first European known to have set foot in Texas did so by accident. Shipwrecked on the coast near Galveston in 1530, Álvar Núñez Cabeza de Vaca wandered among the Indians for six years, finally returning to New Spain, what is now Mexico. Appearing before the Spanish viceroy (governor), he reported rumors of great cities and "signs of gold."[2]

To investigate the rumors, the viceroy sent an expedition in 1540 led by Francisco Vásquez de Coronado. The wealthy cities turned out to be nothing more than poor, dusty Indian pueblos. Coronado, however, was not ready to give up. For two more years he wandered the Southwest, marching through Texas and as far north as Kansas. At last, in April 1542, he abandoned his search and returned to Mexico,

reporting that the land north of the Rio Grande, while good for farming and cattle, contained no wealth. Influenced by his account, Spain made no attempt to settle Texas for the next 150 years.

Coronado's expedition had at least one lasting effect. One of his lieutenants crossed the Texas Panhandle and made contact with a group of Hasinai Indians who referred to themselves as *teychas*, their word for "friends." The Spaniard mistook this for the name of the tribe and called them the "Tejas." Over the years, an "x" was substituted for the "j" and not only the tribe, but also the entire area, became known in Mexico as "Texas," even though its official name was New Philippines.

The French Arrive

The next Texas venture was by a Frenchman, René-Robert Cavelier Sieur de La Salle, who, in 1682, navigated the Mississippi River from Ohio to the Gulf of Mexico. He claimed all the territory for King Louis XIV of France and named it Louisiana. Returning to France, he convinced Louis that "great conquests may be made for the glory of the King, by seizures of provinces rich in silver, and defended

In 1540 Francisco Vásquez de Coronado and his soldiers marched through the Southwest in search of vast cities of gold.

only by a few indolent [lazy] and ennervated [spiritless] Spaniards."[3] He sailed in 1684 with troops, priests, and "some girls seeking husbands."[4]

But, La Salle, though a bold explorer, was a poor navigator. He missed the Mississippi by four hundred miles, landing at Matagorda Bay on the Texas coast. After building a wooden stockade, which he named Fort St. Louis, he and most of the able-bodied men marched east, trying to find their way to the Mississippi. On the way, some of La Salle's men mutinied and he was murdered.

When the Spanish discovered that the French were on Texas soil, they were moved to action for the first time since Coronado. This was the pattern for the next 150 years. Spain was content to leave Texas alone only until another power threatened to take it from them.

Don Alonso de León, governor of the province of Coahuila just south of the Rio Grande, marched up the coast to Fort St. Louis in April 1689 and found only skeletons and desolation. It had been wiped out by Indians. Spain was convinced, however, that a permanent settlement was needed to hold off the French. In 1690, de León returned to the area with four Franciscan friars (members of the Order of St. Francis of Assisi). On the Trinity River, they founded the first mission in Texas, San Francisco de los Tejas, among the Hasinai Indians.

Spain was the only European nation that provided a place for Indians in the social and economic order. The British wanted as little to do with the natives as possible. The French valued them as trading partners but made no real attempt to incorporate them. Spain, however, could not attract colonists in large enough numbers. It needed the Indians to perform the bulk of the labor of farming and mining the silver to be shipped to Spain.

Spanish missionaries preach to Indians. Unlike other European nations, Spain wanted to convert the Mexican natives to Christianity and include them in their social and economic order.

In central Mexico, the Spanish found plenty of settled, agricultural Indian communities. In northern Mexico and in the American Southwest there were no such communities, so the Spanish created missions to gather the Indians together, convert them to Christianity, then teach them to become farmers and herdsmen. A *presidio* (fort) and soldiers were nearby to keep the Indians tame and to protect the mission from more hostile tribes.

The Spanish failed to convert the Hasinai to Christianity or to use them as workers. In 1692, with no further threat from the French on the horizon, the Spanish declared the mission a failure and withdrew to Mexico.

St. Denis

The French soon resumed their efforts, however, and in 1713, the governor of French Louisiana sent a Canadian, Louis Juchereau de St. Denis, to establish an outpost on the Red River. St. Denis named it Natchitoches after the nearby Indians. Once more, the French threat spurred the Spanish into action. They decided to revive the Texas missions as barriers to the French.

In 1716, Spain sent out an expedition that established two *presidios* and several mission churches. One *presidio* was named Nacogdoches (the Spanish spelling for the

Natchitoches) and the other, at the mouth of the Lavaca River, was named La Bahía. Trade between these missions and French Louisiana was strictly forbidden by the Spaniards, although much smuggling took place. Officially, supplies had to come from Mexico, hundreds of miles away. Some sort of settlement was needed in between as a stopping point.

In 1718, a new mission was established as a backup to those in east Texas. The site selected was on a river that in 1692 had

The Alamo

The first Alamo (Mission San Antonio de Valero) was built in 1718. The next year, possibly to get the Indian women away from the soldiers of San Antonio, the Franciscan brothers moved the Alamo to the eastern bank of the San Antonio River. A second building was built, like the first, of adobe— sun-dried bricks of mud and straw. It wasn't until 1727 that the first stone structure was begun on the present site. The principal feature was the chapel, its long, narrow, high-ceilinged nave flanked on either side by smaller rooms. Built in 1744, the chapel collapsed in 1757 and was rebuilt in the form it is seen today.

The chapel faced west. On its north side, a door opened into the cloister, an open area on the west side of which was a two-story building containing the friars' quarters and housing for any guests or soldiers, who might be stationed in the mission if an attack was feared. Beyond this building was a much larger plaza surrounded by stone walls. Along the walls were the houses of the mission Indians, who were locked up at night to prevent them from running away. Outside the walls were the mission's fields, on which the Indians raised crops and tended cattle under the friars' supervision.

The Alamo was never intended to be a fort. Its walls were tall enough (twelve feet) and thick enough (two and a half feet) to resist Indian attacks, but not large cannons. Its walls had no gun platforms. Instead, cannons had to be dragged up earthen ramps onto wooden platforms.

The walls had no parapets running behind them along which men could run and stay out of sight. Neither did they have any holes or battlements from which muskets might be fired. Consequently, if a man fired over the walls, his entire upper body was exposed.

At the time of the Battle of the Alamo, a wall had to be made out of earth and timber to complete the enclosure. It ran from the chapel to the south wall. The total area enclosed by the Alamo walls was about two acres.

been named the San Antonio de Padua. A Franciscan mission in northern Mexico was moved there to convert the local Indians. In honor of the Marqués de Valero, viceroy of New Spain, the mission was christened San Antonio de Valero. Eventually, it would become the Alamo.

In 1721, de Valero sent a troop of fifty-four soldiers to guard the mission and to build a *presidio* nearby. The stone fort, which for some reason was never completed, was named San Antonio de Béxar for de Valero's brother, a Spanish duke. Over time, the entire area containing the fort, the town that grew alongside it, and the string of five missions became known as Béxar.

Eventually, however, the Texas missions failed, unlike those in California and New Mexico. The Coahuiltec Indians around San Antonio de Valero, for instance, refused to be converted. They were unwilling to accept what they considered a harsh code of conduct that went with

Christianity and the punishment that went with breaking the friars' rules. They frequently ran away, and when forced to stay in the missions, lost the will to live. The birthrate decreased. At the high point, about 1750, nearly eight hundred Indians were housed in the five missions of Béxar. Forty years later, there weren't enough left to tend the fields or keep the mission walls in good repair.

The Unconquerable Indians

Indians outside the missions were problems, as well. Unlike the Aztecs of Mexico and the Incas of Peru, the fierce Apaches and Comanches had no cities against which the Spanish could use their cannons. Mounted on swift horses—which they had been stealing from the Spaniards for decades—and using French-supplied firearms, the Apaches and Comanches would swoop down on a settlement, carry

Although undated, this photo of the Alamo remains the earliest known and shows the plaza (left) and the church (right). The Spanish built structures like the Alamo so that missionaries could live and work among the natives.

San Juan Capistrano mission in San Antonio, Texas, was built in 1716. When the Spanish abandoned their Texas missions at the end of the 1700s, most fell into disrepair.

off loot and prisoners, and be gone before resistance could be organized.

Finally, Spain decided to reduce its forces in Texas. The missions were not creating any wealth, and France had yielded Louisiana to Spain in 1762, making the settlements unnecessary from a military standpoint. The only missions remaining in Texas were the five around Béxar and the one at La Bahía, which had been moved from the Gulf Coast to a spot on the San Antonio River about seventy miles southeast of Béxar.

In 1793, these last few missions were shut down. The Franciscans' dreams of a large, peaceful, hardworking Indian population had vanished. At San Antonio de Valero, there were only forty-three settled Indians to show for seventy-five years of effort.

Béxar, however, had grown, and Spain sent more troops to protect settlers from the Indians. In 1801, a cavalry unit arrived from San Carlos del Alamo de Parras in northern Mexico. The commander, shocked that Béxar's *presidio* had never been completed, took over the old San Antonio de Valero mission as his fort. His troops, perhaps homesick for their former post, called their new home the Alamo.

As the 1700s ended, Texas seemed safe from any foreign power, and Spain was once again content to ignore it. More than 250 years of exploration and settlement had left only three thousand Spanish citizens in this vast area larger than Spain itself. Another threat was on the horizon, however, and would come, not from Europe, but from the United States.

The Anglo-Americans reached Texas about 1800, first rogues and adventurers, then settlers by the thousands. A mixture of English, Irish, Scotch, and Germans, they brought with them a culture so alien to that of Spanish Mexico that three decades later the two societies were at war.

Americans who settled in Texas called themselves "Texians," as opposed to the

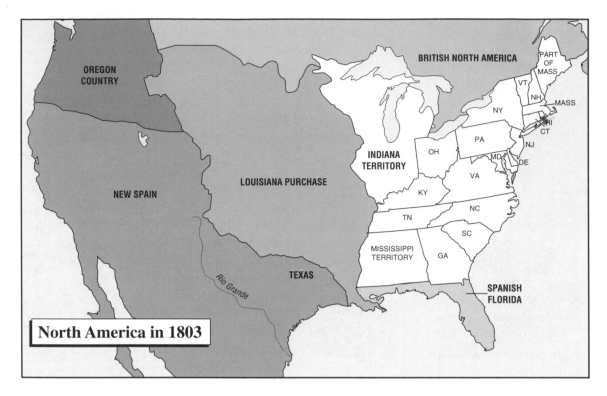

North America in 1803

Tejanos, Mexicans born or living in Texas. The Spanish and Mexicans called them either *nortamericanos* or *anglosajón* (Anglo-Saxon), the latter implying a lack of grace or manners.

The Filibusters

The first Americans to make an impact were the "filibusters," a series of adventurers who ranged across Texas from 1800 to 1820. The word came from the French *fli-bustier*, which in turn was a translation of the English "freebooter," or pirate.

The first filibuster was Philip Nolan, who made a living rounding up wild horses in east Texas and smuggling them into Louisiana. In 1800, he entered Texas with about twenty armed men on what was supposed to be another mustang raid. Actually,

he was secretly in the pay of General James Wilkinson, whose motive was to separate Texas from Mexico and then take it over. Nolan moved as far as the Brazos River before being attacked by a full company of Spanish soldiers. Nolan was killed, and the rest of the Americans surrendered and were marched to Mexico City and imprisoned.

Spain soon had more reason to fear the Americans. In 1803, French dictator Napoleon Bonaparte, having forced Spain to cede Louisiana back to France, sold it to the United States for three million dollars. The United States was now on Texas's doorstep and, even worse, claimed that the Louisiana Purchase extended all the way to the Rio Grande.

Wilkinson negotiated with the Spanish concerning the Texas-Louisiana border. Troops from the two countries were facing each other across a tributary of the Red

River near Natchitoches. To avoid conflict, Wilkinson and the Spanish commander agreed that American forces would pull back seven miles to the Sabine and that the area between them would be the Neutral Ground, where neither country could send troops. Soon, the Neutral Ground was filled with thieves, robbers, and murderers who preyed on settlements in Louisiana and Texas.

Spain, however, had greater problems. In 1810, a priest named Miguel Hidalgo y Costilla launched a revolt in Mexico, which spread rapidly and became a full-scale revolution. Hidalgo's army swelled to eighty thousand men. Though Hidalgo was eventually captured and executed in 1811, his revolution survived him.

Meanwhile, outlaws in the Neutral Ground grew so numerous and bold that a U.S. officer, Augustus Magee, was sent in to clean them out. While there, however, he was contacted by one of Hidalgo's rebels, Bernardo Gutiérrez de Lara. They quickly raised an army made up of Mexican rebels, Americans, Louisiana French, and even some Indians. Although there were some outlaws among them, most of the Americans joined because they firmly believed that Texas should be liberated from the Spanish and become part of the United States.

The Army of the North

In August 1812, this Republican Army of the North crossed into Texas. By April 1813, they had captured Nacogdoches, La Bahía (where Magee died of disease), and San Antonio. On April 6, the Americans drew up a "Declaration of Independence of the State of Texas." They talked of a quick union with the United States.

The Mexicans, however, drew up their own constitution. It did not give liberty to the people, but instead made Gutiérrez and his colleagues absolute rulers instead of the king of Spain. Furthermore, it said that "the State of Texas forms a part of the Mexican Republic, to which it remains inviolably [immovably] joined."[5] Disgusted, many of the leading Americans left for the United States. Without them, the army became a mob.

An American named Henry Perry took command. He managed one victory, but on August 18, 1813, was defeated by an army led by General Joaquín de

Miguel Hidalgo rallies Indian and mestizo revolutionaries to rise up against the government in protest of the treatment they received.

Arredondo. Most of the 850 Americans were killed or executed as were almost all the Mexican revolutionaries. Among Arredondo's troops was an eighteen-year-old lieutenant named Antonio López de Santa Anna Perez de Lebron. Santa Anna saw firsthand the way one deals with rebels—both Mexican and American. He would put those lessons to use twenty-three years later at the Battle of the Alamo.

Santa Anna

Born in 1794, the son of a well-to-do merchant, Santa Anna rejected the efforts of his father to make him a businessman. Declaring that he was not born to be a "counter jumper," he enlisted as a cadet in the Regiment of Vera Cruz at the age of sixteen.

He served with distinction under General Arredondo during the revolt of Hidalgo, including an expedition to Texas in 1813 to punish a mostly North American rebel force. He rose to power as an aide to General Agustín de Iturbide, who made him a general at the age of twenty-seven.

After helping to bring about Iturbide's fall, Santa Anna soon became the most powerful man in Mexico. He became a national hero in 1829 when he defeated the last attempt by Spain to regain control of Mexico at the Battle of Tampico. He was elected president for the first of five times in 1833.

Although his defeat by the Texans in 1836 damaged Santa Anna politically, it by no means ended his career. He soon returned to power and became a hero again when he lost a leg defending Vera Cruz against a French invasion in 1838. He was elected president again in 1841 but was out of power and in exile by the time the Mexican-American War began in 1846.

He hinted to American officials that if restored to power, he might be able to settle differences between the two countries. With American funding, he returned to Mexico and became president once more, only to turn against the United States.

Despite Santa Anna's defeat and Mexico's loss of what would become the entire southwestern part of the United States in the Treaty of Guadalupe Hidalgo in 1848, Santa Anna remained popular. He was forced out of office briefly, but was elected president for the last time in 1853.

He spent most of his remaining years in exile, all the while scheming to get back into power. He finally was allowed to return in 1874 at the age of eighty, feeble, powerless, and penniless. He once refused an operation to improve his sight, saying, "Leave me sunk in darkness. I am more tranquil this way." He died two years later.

In 1819, the DeOnis Treaty was reached whereby the United States acquired Florida in exchange for giving up its title to Texas. This was very unpopular among the citizens of Natchez, Mississippi, who sent an expedition, under the command of Dr. James Long, "to invade Texas and establish a republic."[6] Long eventually was captured, sent to Mexico City, imprisoned, and shot. With his death, the era of the filibusters came to an end.

The filibusters, however, had painted a picture of Texas as a land of opportunity, just waiting for settlers. One who decided to take advantage was Moses Austin, who had moved from Connecticut into Spanish Missouri in 1797 as an *empresario*, one who agreed to bring in a colony. In 1820, wiped out by a bank failure, he rode to San Antonio to try his luck, reasoning that the treaty would cause Spain to open Texas to American settlers.

A Colony Is Approved

The military governor in Monterrey, General Arredondo, had given strict orders that no *nortamericanos* be allowed in Texas. Nevertheless, on January 17, 1821, he sent word that the application had been approved. Arredondo reasoned that the right kind of Americans—permanent settlers—could prevent more expeditions by filibusters and serve as a buffer or shield between the Spanish settlements and the Comanches. By the time word of Arredondo's approval arrived in San Antonio, Moses Austin had started back for home. He died soon after reaching Missouri. On his deathbed he convinced his son, Stephen, to pursue his dream of a Texas colony.

Stephen F. Austin followed his father's dream and founded a permanent American colony in Texas.

Stephen F. Austin spent the summer of 1821 exploring and finally selected a large area of rich land between and on either side of the Brazos and Colorado Rivers. His settlers, the "Old Three Hundred" to which many Texans today proudly trace their family trees, began to arrive that fall and the following spring. Austin, however, was not there. He was in Mexico City, trying to hold on to his colony.

*Stephen Austin issues a land title to Texas colonists in 1822. The vast
majority of these colonists were willing to remain loyal to Mexico.*

The revolution started by Hidalgo had never died out. On September 23, 1821, General Agustín de Iturbide, who had made a deal with the rebels, rode in triumph into Mexico City and declared Mexico a republic. More than three hundred years of Spanish rule had come to an end.

Informed that his grant had been canceled by the new government, Austin hurried to Mexico City. He remained there until 1823. His claim was approved first by Iturbide, who had declared himself emperor, then by a republican congress that overthrew Iturbide with help from his former ally Santa Anna, now a general.

By the time Austin returned to his colony, the number of Texians was about seven thousand, already outnumbering Mexicans by two to one. By 1831 there were twenty thousand. The vast majority were not rebels, but solid, educated, hardworking people, willing to be loyal citizens of Mexico. With them, however, came concepts of self-government totally foreign to the Hispanic tradition of an all-powerful central authority. This was the fundamental cause of the Texas Revolution, and it was made worse by Mexico when it allowed the settlers to rule themselves, frequently ignoring Mexican law.

Cultures in Collision

The two cultures were on a collision course. Nevertheless, the Mexicans continued to allow *empresarios* to bring more settlers in. Most *empresarios* were American, but some were Mexican, including Lorenzo de Zavala and Martín de León. The *Tejanos* had their own problems with the Mexican government. The Constitution of 1824 had combined Texas, which had been a separate province with the capital at San Antonio, with the state of Coahuila. The capital was Monterrey, hundreds of miles to the south. Many prominent *Tejanos* lost much of their influence. San Antonio's population dwindled, troops were withdrawn, and the Alamo fell into disrepair.

The first discord between Texians and Mexico occurred when *empresario* Haden Edwards found that *Tejanos* possessing earlier Spanish grants lived within his colony near Nacogdoches. While Edwards was in the United States on business, Mexican authorities decided disputes in favor of the *Tejanos*. His brother Benjamin complained, and the Edwards grant was revoked.

Furious, Benjamin Edwards proclaimed the "Republic of Fredonia" on December 20, 1826, but he could get no support from his fellow Texians. Austin, in fact, contributed one hundred men to the Mexican force that put down the rebellion and forced Edwards to flee to Louisiana early in 1827.

The American Threat

Despite Austin's help, the Mexican government was more convinced than ever that there was an American plot to take over Texas. On April 6, 1830, a decree was passed forbidding immigration from the United States. Mexican convicts were to be settled in Texas. Customs duties were to be collected to force Texas to trade with Mexico instead of the United States. Texas was to be under the direct supervision of the central government in Mexico City.

The Decree of April 6 was a serious miscalculation on the part of Mexico. Previously, most people had been loyal—the *Tejanos* out of respect for the government and the Texians as long as they were mostly left alone. The new decree changed everything. If Mexico expected obedience, it got protests instead. Meetings were held, first within colonies, then among people of several colonies. Letters were sent to the government. People began to call for Texas to become a state separate from Coahuila. Some of the more hotheaded young Texians even wanted war. It was not far off.

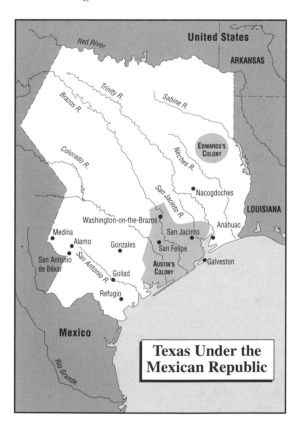

Texas Under the Mexican Republic

Chapter

2 The Rebellion

With the Decree of April 6, 1830, Mexico sought to control American colonists in Texas. Unfortunately for the Mexicans, there was probably no group of people anywhere less willing to be controlled. Their fathers and grandfathers had fought in the American Revolution over similar issues. Also, Americans in Texas tended to be more self-reliant than those who had remained in the United States. Their instinctive desire for independence, plus the inability of Mexico to understand that desire, led to war.

However, the very independence of the Texans (the term for both Texians and the *Tejanos* supporting them) was almost fatal to their cause. Politicians squabbled endlessly among themselves as soldiers begged for help. Men were willing enough to fight, but not to obey orders or submit to army discipline. The resulting series of errors and blunders would end in the tragedy at the Alamo.

Those who protested the Decree of April 6 loudest were late arrivals who found it difficult to obtain land, do business, or practice a profession. One, a twenty-two-year-old lawyer from Alabama named William Barret Travis, was so openly critical of the Mexican commander at Anáhuac on Galveston Bay that he and several others were jailed without charge

William Barret Travis was jailed by the Mexican government for his open and virulent criticism of a Mexican commander.

in June 1832. Although most of the settlers thought Travis somewhat irresponsible, they protested the arrests and demanded the prisoners be freed. Just as mob violence threatened, the commander's superior officer arrived from Nacogdoches, and seeing his troops badly outnumbered, negotiated a settlement.

A brother of one of the prisoners, however, had ridden to San Felipe, capital of Austin's colony, and rounded up a band of hotheads who set out to free the men at Anáhuac by force. They mounted a cannon

Travis

Like many men in Texas in the 1830s, William Barret "Buck" Travis never told anyone exactly why he had come. Once there, however, he became one of the most outspoken, flamboyant leaders of the Texas Revolution. He had always yearned to be a hero, and the Alamo would give him the chance.

Travis was born in 1809 in South Carolina, the oldest son of a farmer. The family moved to Alabama when Travis was nine, but not before he had formed a friendship with James Bonham, two years older, who lived five miles away. They would remain friends until they died together at the Alamo.

Travis was intelligent and an avid reader. By the time he was twenty, he was teaching school and studying law. In 1828, he married Rosanna Cato, one of his pupils, and their son Charles was born the next year. Travis practiced law, published a small newspaper, and had begun to take a role in local politics when he abruptly left for Texas in 1831, abandoning his pregnant wife. No one knows why, but one story, never proved, is that he killed a man who had been Rosanna's lover.

He settled in Nacogdoches and soon had a reputation as a headstrong, impetuous young man who liked to drink, gamble, and womanize when he wasn't practicing law. He wore fancy clothes, a rarity in Texas. When he rode through town on his black horse, he wore a white hat. He kept a diary in crude Spanish, bragging about every woman he made love to.

Rosanna Travis visited her husband early in 1835, bringing their two children with her. She had come to ask Travis either to return to Alabama or to give her a letter with which she could obtain a divorce. She returned with the letter but left young Charles with his father.

Despite Travis's dashing manner and good looks, many people distrusted him. What he considered patriotism, others saw as ambition. He desperately wanted to be a military leader, but men under his command did not seem to respect him, as was shown when James Bowie was overwhelmingly elected by the volunteers at the Alamo as their commander.

The Alamo gave Travis the chance to be the kind of hero he had read about in the novels of the Scottish writer Sir Walter Scott. He had a romantic streak and a vivid imagination that can clearly be seen in the messages he wrote. Whether or not he actually drew the fabled line in the sand, such an action would have been entirely in character.

in a small boat and sailed down the Brazos River, intending to go into the Gulf of Mexico and north to Anáhuac. The mouth of the Brazos, at Velasco, was guarded by a Mexican fort. When the Mexicans refused to let them pass, the Texans fired on the fort and eventually forced it to surrender after most of the Mexican troops had been killed or wounded.

Another Revolution

The so-called Anáhuac War might have drawn a strong response from Mexico, but the Mexican government was shortly thereafter in the grip of another national revolution, this one led by Santa Anna. Since 1821, control of Mexico had gone back and forth between the Federalists, who favored a strong central government, and Republicans, who argued that the states should have a considerable degree of independence. Santa Anna was neither. Instead, as T. R. Fehrenbach writes, he had learned that "the way to high office . . . was not devotion to a soldier's duty but the choice of the proper side."[7]

In 1832, Santa Anna chose to be a Republican and launched a revolution against President Anastasio Bustamante, who was forced to resign. Santa Anna was elected president but cleverly declined to take office, turning it over to his vice president. He claimed he wanted only to return to a simple soldier's life, but in reality knew that whoever was in the president's chair would face serious problems that would make him unpopular.

Texians and *Tejanos* alike were strong supporters of Santa Anna, reasoning they would receive more independence under the Republicans. In fact, Austin was able to prevent Mexican retaliation for the battle at Velasco by claiming the Texans were acting in support of Santa Anna against the representatives of the Federalist government. It was with high hopes, then, that representatives from throughout Texas sent Austin to Mexico City late in 1833 with a proposed constitution for a separate state.

Hispanic governments, however, were not used to being petitioned by their citizens. To the Mexicans, it was a *pronunciamiento*, a formal prelude to a revolt. Austin received a cool reception in Mexico City. Frustrated, he wrote a letter home suggesting Texas go ahead and form its own state government. The letters were intercepted, and Austin was thrown into jail in January 1834. He was to remain there eighteen months.

Santa Anna (pictured) forced Mexican president Anastasio Bustamante to resign after staging a revolt against his government.

FREEMEN OF TEXAS
To Arms!!! To Arms!!!!
"Now 's the day, & now's the hour."

CAMP OF THE VOLUNTEERS,
Friday Night, 11 o'clock;
October 2, 1835.

Fellow Citizens:—

We have prevailed on our fellow citizen Wm. H. Wharton, Esq. to return and communicate to you the following express, and also to urge as many as can by possibility leave their homes to repair to Gonza les immediately, "armed and equipped for war even to the knife." On the receipt of this intelligence the Volun teers immediately resolved to march to Gonzales to aid their countrymen. We are jus now starting which must apol ogize for the brevity of this communi cation. We refer you to Mr. Whar ton for an explanation of our wishes, opinions and intentions, and also for

such political information as has come into our hands. If Texas will now act promptly; she will soon be redeemed from that worse than Egyptian bondage which now cramps her resources and retards her prosperity.

DAVID RANDON,
WM. J. BRYAND,
J. W. FANNIN, Jr.
F. T. WELLS,
GEO. SUTHERLAND,
B. T. ARCHER,
W. D. C. HALL,
W. H. JACK,
WM. T. AUSTIN,
P. D. McNEEL.

P. S. An action took place on yes terdy at Gonzales, in which the Mexi can Commander and several soldiers were slain—no loss on the American side

An 1835 flyer encourages freemen of Texas to take up arms in revolt against Mexico. At first, few settlers supported the revolt.

That spring, with discontent against the government growing, Santa Anna switched sides, took over the presidency, dissolved congress, canceled liberal laws, and began to rule as a dictator. Part of his program was to station more troops in Texas and to renew the taxes imposed in 1830, which had been dropped. He sent a large body of troops to Coahuila, the state bordering Texas on the south, to deal with the uprisings there and to keep an eye on Texas. The commander was General Martín Perfecto de Cós, who had reached his high rank chiefly because he was Santa Anna's brother-in-law.

Trouble in Anáhuac

Once more, it was at Anáhuac that trouble broke out, with Travis once again at the center. In June 1835, Cós sent a rider bearing two messages to the commander, Antonio Tenorio. The public message was that order had been restored in Coahuila and all would be well in Texas. Cós's pri vate message to Tenorio was that rein forcements were on the way and that "the affairs of Texas will definitely be settled."[8]

Unfortunately for Tenorio, some Tex ans seized the rider's saddlebags and made the second message public. The news that troops were on the way spurred the "War Party," as Travis and the other extremists were now called, to action. On June 30, he gathered about two dozen men and one small cannon and marched on the local fort, forcing Tenorio to surrender.

Most Texans were shocked by the acts of Travis and the War Party, which repre sented only a fraction of the settlers. The majority wanted peace and sent representatives to talk with Cós and to proclaim their loyalty to Mexico. Cós responded, however, by moving troops to Matamoros, the Mexican city at the mouth of the Rio Grande, and ordering the arrest of the War Party leaders. Furthermore, he demanded they be arrested by their fellow Texans and turned over to him.

Public opinion, which had been on the side of peace, now swung the other way. No Texan was willing to turn over his fellows to be shot by a firing squad. Communities conducted meetings to prepare to defend themselves against military occupation and martial law. A convention was planned for October 15 at Washington-on-the-Brazos to discuss ways peace could be achieved, and if it could not, to plan for war.

Meanwhile Austin, possibly the only man who could have calmed the situation and maintained peace, had undergone a change of heart. He was released from prison on July 13 and on September 2, sick and disillusioned, reached Texas. When he learned that Cós and his troops had crossed the Rio Grande and were headed for San Antonio, Austin issued a proclamation saying, "War is our only recourse. There is no other remedy. We must defend our rights, ourselves, and our country by force of arms."[9]

Mexican authorities began to prepare for war, too. Cós said publicly that it was time to deal harshly with "foreign settlements in Texas."[10] He reportedly carried with him to San Antonio eight hundred iron shackles in which the rebels would be marched back to Mexico. The Mexicans also began to round up weapons that could be turned against them. One was a six-pounder cannon (so-called because of the weight of the ball it fired) that had

Despite his initial efforts, Stephen Austin could not maintain peace between Texas settlers and the Mexican government.

been given to the people of Gonzales for defense against Indian attacks.

The Start of War

As Cós marched north to San Antonio, the commander there sent Captain Francisco Castañeda and about two hundred men seventy miles east to Gonzales. The citizens there had been asked to surrender the cannon, but vowed not to give it up, burying it instead. Castañeda arrived to find the ferry across the Guadalupe River removed and armed men posted on the eastern bank.

While the Mexicans waited, wondering what to do, armed Texans flocked to Gonzales, including Travis and a twenty-one-year-old West Point dropout named James W. Fannin. They elected John W. Moore their colonel. They decided to attack the Mexicans, dug up the cannon, and put it in the care of a young blacksmith named Almeron Dickinson. When someone suggested a flag was needed, two local women took a piece of white cloth cut from a wedding dress. On it, they painted a star, a crude cannon, and the words "Come and Take It."

Just after dawn on October 2, 1835, the Texans crossed the river and fired the cannon to signal their presence. When Castañeda requested a parley, he and Moore met on horseback between the two lines of troops. Castañeda demanded the cannon; Moore refused. Moore asked Castañeda to join the rebellion; Castañeda, although privately disapproving of Santa Anna, refused and said he would remain and wait for orders. Moore said the Mexicans must withdraw or fight, and on that note, both withdrew.

When Moore reached his line, he waved his hat and cried, "Charge 'em boys, and give 'em hell!"[11] Dickinson fired the cannon in what is traditionally considered the first shot of the Texas Revolution, and the Texans charged. In five minutes, the skirmish was over. Castañeda and his troops fled for San Antonio, leaving two dead. One Texan was slightly wounded.

A week later, another group of Texans defeated the small Mexican garrison at La Bahía, which in 1829 had been renamed Goliad. On October 10, Austin, who had been named general of the Texas army, arrived in Gonzales to take command of what was now a force of about three hundred. Included were Travis, Fannin, and legendary knife fighter James Bowie, who was made a lieutenant colonel. There were no uniforms and little discipline. Men furnished their own weapons, clothes, and horses. One of the soldiers later wrote that the Texans "certainly bore little resemblance to the army of my childhood dreams."[12]

The Siege of San Antonio

The army, now about five hundred after adding recruits along the way, reached San Antonio on November 1. Cós refused to challenge them, despite receiving reinforcements that put his strength at fifteen hundred troops, among which were some of the best in Mexico. Cós probably could have defeated the Texans in a pitched battle, but he was not much of a soldier and elected to stay holed up in San Antonio.

Austin ordered his troops to blockade the city, intending to starve it into surrender. Shortly afterward, he left for a convention of delegates in San Felipe, leaving Colonel Edward Burleson in command. As the army sat, it changed in character. Many of the settlers grew tired of waiting and returned to their farms and families. Their places were taken by volunteers from the United States, eager to fight for liberty and for the free land promised to them.

Meanwhile, at San Felipe, the Consultation, a group of delegates from throughout Texas, was meeting. Both Austin and Sam Houston, a former U.S. congressman who had been in Texas since 1832, argued that to proclaim Texas an independent republic would cost the support of the *Tejanos*. Instead, a government was established for a separate state within Mexico. A council was named, Henry

Smith was elected governor, Houston was named commander in chief of the army, and Austin was sent to the United States to raise money and troops.

At San Antonio, the Texans were growing weary of the blockade. More men slipped away to their homes. Finally, on December 4, Burleson decided to lift the siege and return to Gonzales. The army was almost ready to depart when a Mexican deserter reported that Cós's army was hungry, discouraged, and ripe for defeat. Hearing this, Ben Milam, an old *empresario* who had been run out of Coahuila by Cós, waved his hat and shouted, "Boys! Who will go with old Ben Milam into San Antonio?"[13] Hundreds of men shouted their approval, and Burleson had no choice but to order an attack.

The Battle of San Antonio

The Texans charged into San Antonio at 3 A.M. on December 5, beginning a bloody house-by-house, street-by-street fight that lasted several days. Their goal was the Church of San Fernando, the tallest structure in San Antonio, which served the Mexicans as an observation post and atop which cannons had been placed. Using crowbars to tunnel through connected houses, the Texans reached the church plaza and set up a twelve-pounder cannon, with which they smashed the roof of the church.

Cós now had slightly more than one thousand men, the rest having deserted or been killed. They pulled back from the church and took refuge in the Alamo. For days, the Texas cannons pounded the Alamo walls—the same walls behind which the Texans would be fighting three months later. Finally, Cós raised a white flag and, on December 10, surrendered. He was allowed to return to Mexico, promising first never again to take up arms against Texas. The next day, the Mexicans marched south, leaving their weapons behind.

Up to now, the Texans had kept an enemy in view and a purpose in mind. With the fall of San Antonio, Texas had been swept clear of Mexican soldiers, but the

Riddled with holes made by cannon blasts, a painting entitled El Alamo *shows how the Alamo might have looked during the heated exchange between Mexican general Martin Cós and Texas settlers.*

Texans could not agree on what to do next. They knew Santa Anna would retaliate with an army much larger than theirs, so their best strategy would have been to remain united, build up strong defenses along the semicircle from Goliad to Gonzales to San Antonio, and wait for Santa Anna to cross hundreds of empty miles to reach them. This is precisely what they did not do, and the situation soon dissolved into a farce.

Colonel Frank Johnson, who succeeded Burleson in command of the army at San Antonio, was on fire to carry the war to Mexico—to march south and take Matamoros on the Rio Grande. He was joined by Dr. James Grant, a former aide to Burleson, who had been kicked out of northern Mexico and wanted to get his land back. They were joined by two prominent Mexican liberals, Lorenzo de Zavala and José Antonio Mexía.

The plan split the new government. The Council in San Felipe approved the Matamoros expedition, but it was vetoed by Governor Smith, who distrusted de Zavala and Mexía as "Mexicans who pretend to be our friends."[14] When the Council overruled his veto and ordered the expedition to proceed, Smith called it "caucusing [meeting secretly], intriguing, and corrupt" and said "your services are no longer needed."[15] The Council then voted to remove Smith, but he refused to give up the official seal, promising to "shoot any son of a bitch"[16] who tried to take it from him.

A Government Divided

The Council had not bothered to inform the commander in chief, Houston, of its plans. When it finally told him of the Mata-moros expedition, he approved, but only if it were a small, hit-and-run raid, not an invasion. Nevertheless, the Council went ahead and authorized Johnson to proceed, conferring on him most of Houston's power. Johnson, however, had been talked out of the plan by Governor Smith. The Council, undaunted, transferred command to Fannin, now a colonel. Then, when Johnson changed his mind once more, the Council put him back in command without officially removing Fannin.

At about the same time, Dr. Grant announced that the volunteers in San Antonio had elected him their commander. The Texas army thus had four supreme commanders—Houston, Johnson, Fannin, and Grant—none of whom was bound to take orders from any of the others.

The Mexicans suffered no such division of command. Santa Anna, furious over the fall of San Antonio, resolved to put the Texans in their place for good. He ordered the immediate mobilization of a large army. Even before his brother-in-law's defeat, the Mexican president wrote:

> The foreigners who wage war against the Mexican nation have violated all laws and do not deserve any consideration, and for that reason, no quarter [mercy] will be given them as the troops are to be notified at the proper time. They have audaciously declared a war of extermination to the Mexicans and should be treated in the same manner.[17]

Johnson and Grant, acting on the Council's approval, stripped the Alamo of many of its men and weapons and went to Refugio to concentrate their forces for the march on Matamoros. With them went Fannin, who had little choice since most

Bowie

James Bowie, born in 1796 in Kentucky, came from a no-nonsense background. Soon after the Bowies settled in Louisiana, James's father, Rezin, killed someone trying to trespass on his land. James's mother, accompanied only by a single slave, rode into town and freed her husband at gunpoint.

At the age of eighteen, James was on his own, clearing forests and taking the timber downriver to be sold in New Orleans. It was at this time that he began to acquire a reputation for taming wild horses, hunting wild animals, and amusing himself and friends by riding on the backs of alligators.

About 1819, Bowie sold his land and joined Dr. James Long's filibustering expedition to Texas. After Long's defeat, he went into business with brothers Rezin and John buying African natives from Jean Lafitte, the pirate who had his base on Galveston Island, and smuggling them into Louisiana. While it was legal in the American South to own slaves, it was illegal to import them.

The famous Bowie knife was actually designed by Rezin, who gave it to James to use in a duel. It was designed for fighting, with a guard at the front of the handle to protect the hand and the top of the blade curved and partially sharpened. Bowie used it to kill several opponents, and it became so famous that men asked blacksmiths to make copies. Most of the men at the Alamo probably carried some form of Bowie knife.

In 1828, Bowie moved to Texas, settling in San Antonio and marrying Ursula Veramendi, a daughter of the most prominent *Tejano* family in Texas. He learned Spanish, became a Catholic, and received large grants of land. He was not one, however, to settle down. Late in 1831, he was among a small band of North Americans looking for a lost silver mine near San Saba, Texas, when they were surprised by more than one hundred Indians. After a battle lasting thirteen hours, the Americans escaped with one dead and three wounded. They had killed about forty Indians.

In 1833, Bowie's wife, their two children, and his wife's parents died in a cholera epidemic. This personal loss cut most of Bowie's ties to Mexico, and when trouble began between Mexico and the Texas colonists, he never hesitated in taking the Texans' side, eventually dying at the Alamo.

of his men had decided to go. Lieutenant Colonel James C. Neill was left in command of the Alamo with about one hundred men.

Houston, although he lacked the power to halt the Matamoros expedition, nevertheless went to Refugio to attempt to convince the troops it was a bad idea.

Houston's appeal, plus the news that Santa Anna was sending crack troops to reinforce Matamoros, convinced Fannin, who withdrew to Goliad, taking most of the army—about 420 of the 600 men—with him. Even with most of their troops gone, Johnson and Grant decided to continue the expedition.

Bowie at the Alamo

Houston then turned his attention to the question of what to do with the troops at the Alamo. He sent Bowie, who had been scouring the countryside for recruits, to San Antonio to make a decision whether to try to hold the Alamo or to blow it up and

When Texas settlers decided to invade Mexican territory, Sam Houston tried to convince them that such an expedition would be foolhardy.

bring the forces there east. On February 2, 1836, Bowie wrote to Governor Smith:

> The salvation of Texas depends in great measure on keeping Béxar out of the hands of the enemy. . . . Colonel Neill and myself have come to the solemn resolution that we will rather die in these ditches than give them up. [18]

Smith then ordered Travis, who had managed to get himself appointed a lieutenant colonel, to go to the Alamo and take command. Travis, like Bowie, had been on a recruiting mission but now rode to the Alamo with thirty men. Others came in small groups, some of them volunteers. One such group was made up of a dozen men from Tennessee under the already-famous frontiersman David Crockett, who also brought his trusty rifle "Old Betsy" and a collection of tall tales.

When Smith sent Travis to command the Alamo, he failed to relieve Neill. Neill, who had received word he was needed at home, solved this awkward situation by simply leaving, turning over command to Travis on February 11, the same day Crockett arrived. Most of the soldiers at the Alamo, however, were volunteers who had a tradition of electing their own leader. A vote was taken and Bowie was elected. Travis was disgusted, writing to Governor Smith that Bowie "has been roaring drunk all the time . . . & is proceeding in a most disorderly & irregular manner." [19] Eventually, the two men agreed to share the command.

Santa Anna, meanwhile, had gathered an army and marched for Texas with a speed that would have amazed the Texans—had they known about it. On February 14, one soldier wrote his father that no attack was expected "before a month or

Crockett

Many men became well known as a result of having been at the Alamo, but David Crockett was the only one already famous. After his death, his fame continued to grow, and he remains today, as a result of movies and television, by far the best known of the Alamo defenders.

Crockett was born in 1786 in Tennessee. He did not attend school until he was twelve years old and then only for four days. When his father tried to punish him for fighting, Crockett ran away from home.

After almost three years, Crockett returned and worked for a year to help settle some of his father's debts. He also received six more months of schooling, which he thought would impress a girl he liked. When the romance ended, so did Crockett's education.

In 1806, Crockett married Polly Finley and moved onto a rented farm. As he farmed, he began to gain a reputation as a talented hunter and a dead shot with a rifle. Eventually, the Crocketts would make a series of moves westward, seeking new and better land.

In 1813, Crockett volunteered for the Tennessee militia, commanded by Andrew Jackson, to fight against the Creek Indians. In the same army was a young officer named Sam Houston, but there is no indication the two knew each another.

Shortly after Crockett returned home, his wife Polly died. He soon married again, this time to a widow named Elizabeth Patton. The Crocketts moved again, this time to far western Tennessee. He first got into politics when his neighbors elected him magistrate (something like a justice of the peace). He soon was elected colonel of the county militia and in 1821 was elected to the Tennessee legislature. He was a good campaigner, and enjoyed standing on a tree stump, telling prospective voters tall tales about his hunting.

In 1827, Crockett was elected to the first of three terms in the U.S. Congress. His buckskin clothes and stories about bear hunting caused a sensation in Washington.

Early in his career, he had been a backer of Andrew Jackson and the Democrats, but the two later became political enemies. The Whig Party began a campaign to make Crockett nationally famous and perhaps a challenger to Jackson for the presidency. Within a few years, three books supposedly written by Crockett had been published about his adventures in the wilderness.

In 1835 Jackson's backers went all-out and managed to defeat Crockett in a bitter campaign. Disappointed and frustrated, Crockett told the people of his district, "You can all go to hell. I'm going to Texas." He left only days later on the journey that would take him to the Alamo.

six weeks."[20] Actually, the Mexicans were nine days away at the time. Despite receiving accurate reports about the Mexican army's progress from *Tejanos* friendly to their cause, the Texians dismissed them. The majority of Texians simply did not trust Mexicans, even though several were fighting alongside them.

So when the first wave of Mexican troops reached the Medina River, nine miles from San Antonio, on February 22, the Texians were blissfully unaware. They even held a huge *fandango* (party) in honor of George Washington's birthday that lasted until early the next morning. Santa Anna, in fact, had planned a surprise night attack, and only a heavy rain prevented him from capturing San Antonio with one, quick blow.

The Mexicans Arrive

The Texians awoke on the morning of February 23 to the sound of wagon wheels. The Mexican citizens of San Antonio knew full well how near Santa Anna was and were hurrying to move their families and belongings out of harm's way. At about 1 P.M. a young lookout, Daniel Cloud, was on duty in the bell tower of San Fernando church. He thought he saw something to the south flashing in the sun and rang the alarm bell. Travis scrambled up the staircase. He could see nothing but sent two riders, John W. Smith and Dr. John Sutherland, to take a look.

Following a tradition of electing their own leaders, Texas settlers named Jim Bowie to lead their stand at the Alamo. Bowie was hugely popular, but, unfortunately, rather an unconventional leader.

They had gone about a mile when, coming over a hill, they saw a full regiment of Mexican cavalry. Turning, they rode madly back to the Alamo. Sutherland's horse stumbled in the mud and fell on the doctor, injuring his leg. In great pain, Sutherland remounted and rode on. Long before the two Texians reached the Alamo, Cloud saw both of them as well as the Mexicans. Frantically, he rang the alarm bell again. The Battle of the Alamo had begun.

Chapter

3 The Siege: First Week

The arrival of Mexican troops at San Antonio on Tuesday, February 23, 1836, set off a mad scramble by the Texans to get inside the Alamo, the only structure resembling a fort. With most of his army still on the march, Santa Anna lacked both the men and the cannons to take the old mission by storm. Instead, he began to encircle it, trying to shut off supplies and reinforcements, waiting for the rest of his troops. It would be thirteen long days before he felt strong enough for an all-out assault, days during which the Texans looked in vain for help.

About half the Texans were quartered in the city, not in the Alamo. Others, normally in the Alamo, were still sleeping off the effects of the previous night's *fandango*. When the alarm bell sounded, they grabbed their weapons and whatever else they could carry and headed for the mission. Almeron Dickinson, the Gonzales blacksmith-turned-gunner, had his wife, Susannah, and baby daughter with him. Mounting his horse, he shouted, "Give me the baby! Jump on behind and ask me no questions."[21] Jim Bowie, who had married into a prominent *Tejano* family, brought his two sisters-in-law. Someone had enough presence of mind to round up thirty head of cattle. Others carried in sacks of grain.

One of Travis's first acts was to send for help. During the siege, he would dispatch sixteen couriers, all pleading for aid. A week before, he had sent Lieutenant James Bonham, a boyhood acquaintance in Alabama, to Goliad asking

William Barret Travis (pictured) shared the command of the Texans at the Alamo with Jim Bowie.

Susannah Dickinson

Susannah Wilkerson, born in Tennessee in 1814, was only fifteen when she ran away from home to marry Almeron Dickinson, a young blacksmith originally from Pennsylvania. In 1831, the couple settled in Gonzales, Texas, and their daughter, Angelina, was born there in 1834.

Almeron Dickinson fired what is traditionally called the first shot of the Texas Revolution on October 2, 1835, using a cannon that Mexican authorities had demanded be returned. Dickinson then went on to the Battle of San Antonio with the Texas army. After the victory, he sent for his wife and child, the only man from Gonzales known to have done so.

When Santa Anna and his troops arrived on February 23, 1836, Susannah and her daughter were taken by Almeron Dickinson to the Alamo. She and Angelina were the only female Anglo-Americans there. After the battle, slightly wounded, she was sent by Santa Anna to warn the rest of Texas against further resistance.

Although she was considered a heroine and was constantly sought after to tell her story of what happened at the Alamo, Susannah Dickinson received virtually no assistance from the Republic of Texas. She received her husband's allotment of land, but her appeals for financial help were ignored.

Her life after the war was one failed marriage after another. Her second husband beat her severely, her third was an alcoholic, and her fourth divorced her for adultery. Finally, she settled down with a fifth husband, a cabinetmaker from Germany, and became respectable.

Late in her life, she went on a tour of the Alamo, which had been allowed to fall into disrepair. Seeing one room, she exclaimed, "My God. This was a hospital room. Fifteen Texans were murdered in this room, and now it is full of garbage." Thanks in part to her efforts, the Alamo was saved and restored.

The story of Angelina Dickinson, "Babe of the Alamo," was even more sad. In 1843, some Texas senators tried to secure a pension for her, but they were voted down by newcomers to whom the Battle of the Alamo meant little. Angelina married at sixteen, was divorced, and eventually became a prostitute. She died in 1869, fourteen years before her mother.

Fannin to send reinforcements. Now, with the Mexicans on his doorstep, Travis's messages became more urgent. He wrote another quick note to Fannin and sent it on its way with a man named Johnson. He wrote another saying, "We have 150 men and are determined to defend the Alamo to the last. Give us assistance."[22] He first

Bonham

Like his boyhood friend William B. Travis, James Bonham yearned to be the kind of hero he read about in books. And, like Travis, he was to find his chance at fame in the Alamo.

He was born in 1807, the fifth child of a successful planter in South Carolina. He received a good education but was something of a troublemaker in school. It seemed to people as if he were a born rebel.

This wild streak came out later when Bonham was a student at South Carolina College. Angered by poor food and a rule that students must attend classes even in bad weather, he organized a protest at which he appeared dramatically dressed entirely in black. He was expelled, but continued to study privately and became an attorney in 1830.

He soon found another cause, high customs duties imposed by the federal government. The governor of South Carolina vowed to not pay the duties, and called out the state militia, appointing Bonham a lieutenant colonel. For several months, Bonham got to wear a flashy uniform with a red sash. Then, a compromise was reached, and he had to return to his law practice.

He continued to be a rebel. In 1833, when a man insulted a woman client of his, Bonham thrashed him with a cane. When a judge rebuked him, Bonham threatened to pull his nose. He was sentenced to three months in jail but lived there like a king, showered with gifts and food by the women of the town.

He left South Carolina after a disappointing love affair and opened a law practice in Montgomery, Alabama. He was unhappy there, and the law seemed dull to him. Then, he got another chance to be a rebel. Travis wrote him that these were "stirring times" in Texas. Bonham closed his law office, bid good-bye to his family in South Carolina, and headed to Texas.

Once in Texas, Bonham was used mainly to recruit troops, something at which he excelled. Unlike Travis, men liked Bonham and eagerly followed him. At the Alamo, he was Travis's most trusted messenger. He demonstrated his courage and won a place among Texas heroes by returning to the Alamo, knowing it would almost certainly mean his death.

addressed it to a judge in Gonzales, then scratched out the judge's name and wrote, "To any of the inhabitants of Texas." This was entrusted to Sutherland and Smith.

As Johnson rode toward Goliad, he met Bonham coming the other way. Fannin had refused to send reinforcements, and Bonham was returning to the Alamo with the bad news. Johnson continued toward Goliad. Surely, he thought, Fannin would help once he found out the Texans were actually under siege. Bonham rode on to San Antonio and slipped into the Alamo.

Crockett, who had said he wanted to be a "high private" rather than an officer, now told Travis, "Colonel, here I am. Assign me a position and I and my twelve boys will try and defend it."[23] The Tennesseans were assigned possibly the most dangerous post of all, the wooden palisade on the southwest corner of the chapel.

By 3 P.M. all the Texans were in the Alamo, and the Mexicans had overrun San Antonio. From the top of the tower of San Fernando church they hung a solid red flag. This was the sign that no quarter would be given, no prisoners taken, no mercy shown. Travis knew what the red banner meant and impulsively answered it with a shot from his eighteen-pound cannon, the largest in the Alamo and, for that matter, in all of Texas. The Mexicans answered with a few shells that exploded in the Alamo plaza, doing no harm.

"The Rebellious Foreigners"

Before the cannon shot, the Mexicans had sounded a bugle call requesting a meeting. Travis had not realized what the bugle call meant, but Bowie had and was furious at Travis for firing the cannon without consulting him. Bowie wrote a message requesting negotiations and sent it with his aide to the Mexicans. One of Santa Anna's aides replied that "the Mexican army cannot come to terms under any conditions with the rebellious foreigners."[24] As Bowie's messenger returned, another left the Alamo, this one sent by Travis, angry because Bowie had not consulted him before sending his message. Travis's man received the same reply.

This squabbling between the two commanders was almost over. On the morning of February 24, Bowie was seriously ill, possibly with pneumonia. One story said he collapsed after helping heave a cannon into place. He handed over sole command of the Alamo to Travis. Meanwhile,

Travis reviews his troops at the Alamo. Sharing the command with Bowie, Travis was in almost constant conflict with his fellow commander.

Santa Anna's troops dug trenches about four hundred yards to the west of the Alamo, behind which their first two batteries (groups of cannons) were placed. The guns were too light—the heaviest an eight-pounder—to do much damage against the thick walls, but they did manage to knock the Texans' eighteen-pounder from its mounting, although it was quickly repaired.

As night fell, Travis wrote his most famous appeal:

> To the People of Texas and All Americans in the World—Fellow Citizens and Compatriots: I am besieged with a thousand or more of the Mexicans under Santa Anna. I have sustained a considerable Bombardment and cannonade for 24 hours and have not lost a man. The enemy has demanded surrender at discretion, otherwise the garrison is to be put to the sword, if the fort is taken. I have answered the demand with a cannon shot, and our flag still waves proudly from the wall. *I shall never surrender or retreat.* Then, I call on you in the name of Liberty, of patriotism, and everything dear to the American character, to come to our aid with dispatch. The enemy is receiving reinforcements daily and will no doubt increase to three or four thousand in four or five days. If this call is neglected I am determined to sustain myself as long as possible and die like a soldier who never forgets which is due his honor and that of his country. VICTORY OR DEATH.[25]

This message was given to Albert Martin, who slipped out the gate and rode east through the dusk toward San Felipe.

A Serenade

There was little sleep for the Texans that night or any night during the siege. Santa Anna ordered his military bands to move as close to the Alamo as they dared and play music in order to keep those inside awake. The music was punctuated with an occasional grenade lobbed over the wall by a small cannon.

On the morning of February 25, the Mexicans attempted a sudden rush against the south side of the Alamo. Crossing the river to the south, about two hundred soldiers made their way through La Villita, a hodgepodge of poor shacks and huts. When they reached open ground about one hundred yards from the mission, the Texans' cannons erupted, spewing forth a deadly hail of grapeshot (small iron balls) supplemented with scrap metal and chopped-up horseshoes. Crockett's "boys" opened fire with their long squirrel rifles; the Mexicans were easy targets at such close range for these seasoned hunters.

The Mexicans halted, then fell back into La Villita, taking shelter among the houses. Travis knew now he had made a mistake in not destroying La Villita. He called for volunteers. A short time later, Charles Despallier and Robert Brown dashed across the open space carrying torches. Covered by rifle fire from inside the Alamo, the two men set fire to the huts, which—made mostly of dry sticks and mud—were soon blazing away. Despallier and Brown zigzagged back to the Alamo gate, amazingly untouched by a hail of Mexican bullets.

That night, there was no serenade. At 9 P.M. a "norther," a bitterly cold north wind, blew in, dropping the temperature

Mexican troops storm the south wall of the Alamo. Just to the left of the chapel is the wooden palisade defended by the Tennessee volunteers under David Crockett.

below freezing. Travis wrote another dispatch, this one to Houston, who had spent most of February fashioning a treaty with the Cherokee Indians to prevent them from attacking Texas settlements while the Texans were occupied with Mexico. "If they [the Mexicans] overpower us," Travis wrote, "we fall a sacrifice at the shrine of our country, and we hope prosperity and our country will do our memory justice. Give me help, oh my country." [26]

To carry this message, he chose Captain Juan Seguin, a prominent *Tejano*, and Seguin's aide Antonio Cruz y Arocha. Seguin borrowed a horse from Bowie, who was so ill he barely recognized his old friend. Riding through the night along the road to the east, the pair encountered a dismounted Mexican patrol, huddling around their fire. The couriers were challenged, but answered in flawless Spanish. The patrol relaxed, thinking it was an officer making his rounds. When they reached the patrol, however, Seguin and Cruz y Arocha spurred their horses into a run. Startled, the Mexicans fired at them, but missed.

The Sharpshooter

When the sun rose on February 26, the Texans discovered that the Mexicans had been busy through the night, taking advantage of the darkness to dig more trenches. Their new batteries were to the southwest of the Alamo and a hundred yards closer. The defenders had work of their own to do. The walls of the Alamo had been damaged during the battle in December, and the Texans' engineer, Green B. Jameson, directed the men in packing earth against the weak spots. Mexicans still lurked in the remaining La

Seguin

The story of Juan Seguin was like that of most of the *Tejanos* who fought alongside the North Americans during the Texas Revolution. Once the war was won and waves of immigrants began arriving from the United States, they found themselves unwanted in the country they had helped bring about.

Seguin was from a wealthy and influential family. His father had been a delegate to the national congress of 1824, and Juan served as *alcalde* (mayor) of San Antonio several times, the first when he was only eighteen. He welcomed the arrival of North American settlers and agreed with them that Texas should become a separate state within Mexico.

When the fighting broke out, Seguin recruited a company of *Tejano* volunteers. He fought during the Battle of San Antonio and was in the Alamo when Santa Anna began the siege. He escaped being killed only because he had been sent out by Travis as a messenger.

After the fall of the Alamo, Seguin joined Sam Houston and commanded a company at the Battle of San Jacinto. Soon afterward, he was promoted to colonel and put in command of the San Antonio area. He was elected to the Texas senate in 1838 and elected mayor of San Antonio in 1840.

Texas was becoming full of new settlers, however, most of whom distrusted *Tejanos*. Seguin was falsely accused of betraying a Texas military expedition to New Mexico and was forced from office in 1842. He fled to Mexico and was arrested, but later was drafted into the army. He became an officer and fought against Texas in border disputes and against the United States in the Mexican-American War.

After the war, he received permission to return to Texas and lived quietly on a ranch until 1867, when he moved to land he owned in Mexico. He died in 1890.

Although Juan Seguin remained loyal to the cause of Texas independence, Texans did not remain loyal to him.

Back at the Alamo, Commander Travis sent word for reinforcements to James Fannin, commander of the mission at Goliad (pictured).

Villita huts but hesitated to expose themselves to rifle fire. Captain Rafael Soldana later described a man "with flowing hair," whose aim was so accurate that "we all learned to keep at a good distance when he was seen to make ready to shoot. . . . This man I later learned was known as 'Kwockey' [Crockett]."[27]

The next day, Saturday, saw little action. A squad of Mexicans tried to dam a small stream to the north to cut off the Alamo's water supply. They didn't realize that the Texans had a well. That night, Santa Anna wrote to General Vicente Filisola, who was still marching north, that "they [the Texans] still act stubborn, counting on the strong position which they hold and hoping for much aid from their colonies and from the United States, but they shall soon find out their mistake."[28]

Travis was writing, too. He had sent his first pleas for reinforcements from the Alamo on Tuesday. Now, it was Saturday night. Not only had no help arrived, but Travis had received no word at all from outside. Had any of his messages gotten through? Where was Fannin? Even though Bonham had told him Fannin was not coming, Travis decided to send Bonham to Goliad once more.

The Alamo's messengers had, in fact, gotten through, but Fannin was not coming. On February 25, Johnson had arrived with Travis's first message. Although Fannin had told Bonham only days earlier that he would not bring troops to the Alamo, the news that Santa Anna and the main body of his army were in San Antonio changed his mind, although he still had doubts. "I am well aware that my present move towards Béxar is anything but a military one," he wrote. "The appeals of Cols. Travis and Bowie cannot however pass unnoticed . . . much must be risked to relieve the besieged."[29]

It took Fannin the better part of three days to prepare to march 320 men to San Antonio, leaving about 100 behind to guard the old Goliad mission, which the men had renamed "Fort Defiance." The Texans had plenty of weapons, including four small cannons, but were short of clothing and food. They also lacked horses and were forced to use oxen to pull the baggage wagons.

A Short Journey

Finally, on Sunday morning, February 28, the troops left Fort Defiance for San Antonio. They had gone only a few hundred yards when a wagon broke down. Everything stopped while it was repaired. When they reached the river, two more wagons had to be fixed. Then it was discovered that the oxen had to be unhitched from the wagons and yoked together to drag the cannons across the high water. By the time the crossing had been made, both the oxen and men were exhausted. Furthermore, the river was so high that the ammunition wagon could not cross without the danger of ruining all the gunpowder. Fannin decided to camp for the night by the river. The Texans had gone less than a mile from Goliad.

The next morning, the oxen were missing. They had been turned loose to graze, and no one had been assigned to guard them. Most of the day was spent rounding them up. Frustrated and disheartened, Fannin called a meeting of his officers. As usual, he was indecisive. Basically, he thought the march to the Alamo was a bad idea, but how could he ignore Travis's call for help? His mind was made up for him when a courier rode up with fearful news. Two days earlier, the ill-fated Matamoros expedition under Johnson and Grant had been defeated by Mexican cavalry troops under General José Urrea. Fannin was convinced Urrea would now advance on Goliad. He issued the necessary orders, and the entire column recrossed the river and creaked back into Fort Defiance.

Not all of Travis's appeals went unheeded. Late on the afternoon of February 24, Sutherland and Smith reached

Although Travis had sent several desperate messages to James Fannin (pictured) requesting reinforcements, Fannin failed to come to the Alamo's aid.

Gonzales. Their news from the Alamo electrified the little town. It was proud of having been the site of the first battle of the revolution and was willing to do more. Only the day before, the men had organized the Gonzales Ranging Company of Mounted Volunteers, and elected George Kimball, a hatmaker from New York, to command them. Now, instead of staying home to guard the town, they prepared to ride to San Antonio.

At 2 P.M. on February 27, the volunteers made their farewells to friends and families in the town square and rode west. There were only twenty-five of them, and they would pick up seven more on the way. They were guided by Smith, who had brought the message from Travis. Albert Martin, who had ridden with Travis's "Victory or Death" dispatch was there, eager to return to the Alamo. Isaac Millsaps, at forty-one, was the oldest, leaving behind a blind wife and seven children. The youngest were Johnnie Gaston and Galba Fuqua, only sixteen. They were all aware of the situation at the Alamo and must have known they were going to their deaths.

The Alamo Cannons

As with most things about the Battle of the Alamo, there is disagreement over exactly how many cannons the Texans had available to defend the old mission against Santa Anna's army. The real question, however, is not how many there were but how they were used.

There is little doubt that most of the artillery in Texas was concentrated at the Alamo. Some cannons had been there for years, some had been captured from General Cós in the December battle, and some were brought in by the Texans. Altogether, there were probably more than thirty pieces.

The trouble was that only about twenty were mounted and ready for use. By far the largest was the eighteen-pounder at the southwest corner, capable of firing an iron ball even beyond the western limit of San Antonio. It would have done the Texans no good, however, to batter down houses and would have instead been a waste of powder. The cannons were needed against men, not buildings.

Next in size were the three twelve-pounders mounted at the east end of the chapel and one on the west wall. As things turned out, the cannons in the chapel played only very minor roles in the battle. Much more use was made of the twelve-pounder on the west wall and the five eight-pounders on the north wall. A collection of smaller cannons, six-pounders and four-pounders, along the south and east walls completed the Alamo's artillery.

It might have been possible for the Texans to rig mounts for some of the cannons that were not in use, but the problem wasn't a shortage of cannons. It was a shortage of men to fire them. For instance, the full crew for a twelve-pounder, as called for in military manuals, was fifteen, including gunner, loaders, rammers, spongemen, ventmen, and "powder monkeys" to fetch powder from where it was stored. The Texans probably got by with fewer than half the number prescribed. To man each gun fully would have taken almost every defender in the Alamo.

In addition, a full crew was necessary only if a cannon was to be used for maximum efficiency—that is, fired as often as possible. The men of the Alamo had neither the powder nor the ammunition for sustained firing.

Tightening the Noose

Meanwhile, Santa Anna was tightening the noose around the Alamo. New batteries had been placed to the southeast and northeast. During the day, they pounded away at the walls. At night, the Mexicans dug trenches and piled up earthworks so that with each dawn, the cannons had been moved a little closer. Most of the Mexican cavalry under Joaquín Ramírez y Sesma patrolled the area to the east, both to watch for Texan reinforcements and to prevent the men in the Alamo from escaping. Although the troopers could probably have stopped a mass exodus, they were spread too thin to prevent scouts and messengers from slipping in or out.

Spirits inside the wall remained high. As of February 29, the Texans had been under siege a week but had not lost a man. The only wounds were a few scratches inflicted by stone chips sent flying by cannonballs. They had plenty of water and food, although the only food was beef and corn. They were holding fast, killing a fair share of the enemy, and hoping that the help they were counting on would arrive soon.

To be sure, there was almost no chance to sleep. There were so few men in the Alamo, about 150 at this point, that every man was needed on the walls. They tried to nap curled up next to their rifles and cannons, ignoring the music blaring at them most nights from the Mexican bands. On the night of February 28, they even had a little music of their own. Crockett found an old fiddle and challenged John McGregor, a Scot who had brought along his bagpipes, to a musical duel.

Just after midnight on Tuesday, March 1, the volunteers from Gonzales stole silently, single file, toward the Alamo from the east. Smith, who had lived in Béxar for years and knew the countryside well, led them through thickets of mesquite trees and down gullies, listening for Mexican patrols. Suddenly, a horseman appeared in front of them and a voice said in English, "Do you wish to go into the fort, gentlemen?" Smith hesitated; something—he didn't know exactly what—was wrong. He shouted, "Boys, it's time to be after shooting that fellow."[30] Before any of the Texans could raise their guns, however, the stranger spurred his horse and vanished.

At last, the Texans reached the Alamo. They were spotted by a sentry, who didn't wait to find out their identity before firing his rifle. One of the Gonzales men, hit in the foot, yelled out a curse so obviously American that there was no doubt the newcomers were friends. The main gate on the south wall opened to admit them, and they received a joyful welcome. Several men inside the fort, such as Almeron Dickinson, were from Gonzales and greeted their old friends with hugs and backslaps.

Travis rushed from his quarters, no doubt hoping that Fannin had arrived with four hundred soldiers or Sam Houston with even more. Instead, he found only thirty-two tired, hungry men. He still had fewer than two hundred troops with which to hold off Santa Anna. Still, if the thirty-two men had made their way into the Alamo, others could follow. The next day might bring Fannin into view. Travis had no way of knowing that the thirty-two members of the Gonzales Ranging Company of Mounted Volunteers were the first, last, and only reinforcements the Alamo would ever receive.

4 The Siege: Second Week

As the siege of the Alamo wore on, the strength of the Mexican army increased daily. The mission was under fire from gun emplacements on every side except the east, where companies of cavalrymen patrolled to cut off any escape. Neither the Texans nor Santa Anna had made any offer of surrender. Travis still hoped Fannin would come from Goliad with reinforcements. Santa Anna was waiting for the right opportunity to destroy the Alamo and the Texans with it.

Tuesday, March 1, was cold and damp. The Texans were running low on both gunpowder and cannonballs. They had thought gunpowder was plentiful, since a large supply had been captured from Cós in December, but it proved to be of poor quality—"little more than charcoal dust."[31] Travis had given orders that powder and ammunition be used only when the Alamo was under attack. On this day, however, a promising target presented itself. The Músquez house on the main plaza of San Antonio was the scene of unusual activity, officers coming and going. Could this be Santa Anna's headquarters? Travis decided that it was, literally, worth a shot.

Two of the twelve-pounders on the west wall were fired. One ball missed, but the other smashed into the house. It was, in fact, Santa Anna's headquarters, but he was not there. He was at an old mill north of the Alamo where a battery had been placed. Colonel Juan Almonte noted in his diary that when *el presidente* returned to find his house a shambles, he was angry for the rest of the day.

On the same day, Bonham reached Goliad to deliver one last appeal to Fannin. It was refused. Fannin was certain that Urrea's troops would come any day. He urged Bonham to stay in Goliad. To return

Despite the efforts of James Bonham (pictured), Fannin could not be persuaded to send reinforcements to the Alamo.

Fannin

Although he was only twenty-one years old, James Fannin had more formal military training than anyone in the Texas army. Ironically, he had no faith in his ability to command and his inability to make critical decisions would play a tragic role in the Texas Revolution.

He was born in Georgia in 1805, the illegitimate son of Dr. Isham Fannin, a wealthy planter. He was rejected by his father and raised by his mother's father, James Walker, under the name James Fannin Walker.

It was by that name that he was admitted to the U.S. Military Academy at West Point when he was only fourteen years old. He was a good student and ranked sixteenth in a class of eighty-six when, after a fight with a fellow cadet, he left West Point after two years.

He returned to Georgia in 1821, changed his name to James Walker Fannin, married, and had two children. What he did to make a living is unknown, but he evidently was not very good at it. In 1834, with money borrowed from friends, he moved his family to Texas.

Fannin settled at Velasco on the coast near the mouth of the Brazos River. He operated a plantation, but his chief occupation was the slave trade, illegally importing African natives for sale in the United States.

He was one of the leaders, along with William Travis and James Bonham, of the "War Party" and on a trip to the United States in 1835 told Major Francis Belton that "a few experienced officers" would shortly be needed. When Texas delegates met that October, Fannin proposed that West Pointers be brought in to organize military operations.

When war broke out, Fannin was appointed a captain. He fought at Gonzales and San Antonio, eventually became a colonel, and was one of four "supreme commanders" appointed by various squabbling factions in the Texas government early in 1836.

He wound up commanding the largest force in Texas, about five hundred men at Goliad, but proved unable to make decisions—whether to go to the aid of the Alamo or retreat in the face of the Mexican advance—until it was too late. He also was undecided about his fitness for command. Several times, he wrote to the Council to remove him from his post. In one letter, he said, "I am a better judge of my military abilities than others, and if I am qualified to command an Army, I have not found it out."

Members of the convention at Washington-on-the-Brazos listen as the Texas Declaration of Independence is read. The meeting would be interrupted by yet another appeal from Travis to send reinforcements to the Alamo.

to San Antonio, he said, would mean certain death. "I will make my report to Travis or die in the attempt,"[32] Bonham answered. He spat on the ground, mounted his horse, and rode off, leaving Fannin alone with his conscience.

Not everyone at Goliad agreed with their commander. Many had friends and relatives in the Alamo and wanted to attempt a rescue, however slim their chances. Private Joseph Ferguson wrote to his brother that

> the majority of the soldiers don't like him [Fannin], for what reason I don't know, unless it is because they think that he has not the interest of the country at heart, or that he wishes to become great without taking the proper steps to achieve greatness.[33]

The Convention

Meanwhile, at the tiny town of Washington-on-the-Brazos, more than 150 miles to the northeast, representatives from all over Texas were meeting to form a new government. Among them were two men, Samuel Maverick and Jesse Badgett, who had been elected at the Alamo on February 5 to represent the Texans there. Word of the Alamo siege had arrived on February 29 and created some excitement, but evidently not as much as the arrival of Sam Houston, back from a month with the Cherokee. One observer wrote, "Gen'l Houston's arrival has created more sensation than that of any other man."[34]

The convention formally began on March 1, and on the next day a declaration

UNANIMOUS

DECLARATION OF INDEPENDENCE,

BY THE

DELEGATES OF THE PEOPLE OF TEXAS,

IN GENERAL CONVENTION,

AT THE TOWN OF WASHINGTON,

ON THE SECOND DAY OF MARCH, 1836.

[Body of the declaration reproduced in facsimile.]

RICHARD ELLIS, President.

[Signatures of the delegates, grouped by municipality.]

The Texas Declaration of Independence in its final form. The first version was so full of typographical and grammatical errors it was sent back to the committee for redrafting.

of independence was read and approved. When a copy was presented for signing, however, it was so full of spelling, grammar, and punctuation errors that it had to be sent back to a committee for correction. In its final form, it read:

> We, therefore, the delegates, with plenary [absolute] powers, of the people of Texas, in solemn convention assembled, appealing to a candid world for the necessities of our condition, do hereby resolve and declare, that our political connection with the Mexican nation has forever ended, and that the people of Texas do now constitute a FREE, SOVEREIGN, and INDEPENDENT REPUBLIC and are fully invested with all the rights and attributes which properly belong to independent nations; and, conscious of the rectitude [integrity] of our intentions, we fearlessly and confidently commit the issue to the

supreme Arbiter [judge] of the destinies of nations.[35]

The delegates' work at Washington-on-the-Brazos was not complete. When they met on March 3, they still had to write a constitution and elect a government. All work came to a halt, however, when a courier arrived from Gonzales with Travis's "Victory or Death" message. The convention hall, an unpainted wooden warehouse that lacked even glass windows, was filled with shouts of men ready to spring on their horses and head for the Alamo. Houston calmed them down, telling them that much of their present predicament came from lack of organization. They must stay, he said, until their work was finished. Both Houston and the delegates probably knew that they could not reach San Antonio in time to be of any help. They didn't even bother to try. Houston would later ruefully admit that the delegates "signed the constitution on my birthday [March 3] and had a great spree on egg nog [laced with whiskey] for two days!"[36]

As it turned out, the delegates were correct. On March 3, General Antonio Gaona arrived in San Antonio with a thousand men and ten more cannons. Santa Anna now had twenty-four hundred troops surrounding the Alamo. Still, one last rider was able to make his way inside. It was Bonham, who had ridden almost nonstop from Goliad with the news that there would be no help from Fannin.

An Offer of Surrender

Travis now knew that his situation was virtually hopeless. Two Mexican accounts of the battle claim that he secretly sent an offer to Santa Anna to surrender, providing the men's lives were spared. General Filisola later wrote that the offer was refused "since there are no guarantees for traitors."[37]

But Travis had not completely given up hope. He wrote a letter to the convention in Washington-on-the-Brazos and sent it out with Smith. In addition to an appeal for troops, he urged the convention delegates to

make a declaration of independence, and we will then understand, and the world will understand, what we are fighting for. If independence is not declared, I shall lay down my arms, and so will the men under my command. But under the flag of independence, we are ready to peril our lives a hundred times a day.[38]

Smith also would carry with him personal messages from many of those inside the Alamo, including one from Travis to David Ayers, in whose care Travis's son had been placed. "Take care of my little boy," it read. "If . . . I should perish, he will have nothing but the proud recollection that he is the son of a man who died for his country."[39]

Perhaps Travis suspected that a major attack by the Mexicans was not far off. He told Smith that the huge eighteen-pounder, whose roar could be heard as far away as Gonzales, would be fired three times a day—dawn, noon, and sunset—to let those within earshot know that the Alamo still stood.

It was almost midnight when Smith left. Earlier, one of the best-known and most controversial events in the Battle of the Alamo supposedly took place—Travis's line in the sand. Historians argue whether or not it ever happened. None of the survivors, such as Susannah Dickinson or Joe, Travis's black servant, ever mentioned it. On the other hand, the person who told the story afterward, Louis Rose, was the very person whose reputation it would harm the most.

According to the story, Travis assembled all his men—somewhere between 180 and 200—in the Alamo plaza. He told them formally what most already knew: Fannin would not be coming. He said an all-out assault by the Mexicans could be expected any day and that "we must sell our lives as dearly as possible."[40] Travis said he was willing to stay and die but would not force anyone else to do so. Drawing his saber, he walked across the plaza, scratching a line in the sand. Any man who wished to stay in the Alamo, he said, should cross the line.

Some versions of the story claim that it was a man named Tapley Holland who first crossed over. Others say it was Crock-ett. All mention that Jim Bowie was there on his cot, too ill to stand. "Boys," he supposedly said, "I am not able to go to you, but I wish some of you would be so kind as to remove my cot over there."[41]

The Last Man

Finally, only one man, Rose, was left. Over fifty, he was one of the oldest men in the Alamo and had been a soldier most of his life, having fought for Napoleon Bonaparte in France thirty years earlier. He was a survivor, not a hero. "You seem not to be willing to die with us, Rose," said Bowie.

"No," Rose said, "I am not prepared to die, and I shall not do so if I can avoid it."

"You may as well die with us, old fellow," said Crockett, "for you cannot escape."[42]

Rose gathered his belongings, slipped over the wall, and dropped to the ground

Knowing that the hope for reinforcements was futile, Travis draws a line in the sand, asking all who wish to take a last stand with him to cross it.

Rose

One of the most hotly debated stories surrounding the Battle of the Alamo is the line in the sand supposedly drawn by William Barret Travis. The only source for the story was Louis Moses Rose, who later claimed to have refused to cross the line and then to have escaped.

Susannah Dickinson, who survived the battle, remembered that the night before the final assault, Travis asked anyone who wished to leave to step forward. One man did. "His name to the best of my recollection was Ross," she said. "The next morning he was missing." There is no record of anyone by that name at the Alamo.

Because neither Mrs. Dickinson nor any other survivor, besides Rose, mentioned the line in the sand, critics have charged that he invented the story. It is difficult, however, to see why any person would make up a story that cast him in such an unfavorable light.

After the war, Rose settled in Nacogdoches, Texas, and opened a meat store. Because of his reputation as "the only coward at the Alamo," his business failed. He made no secret of his past and, when asked why he had fled, would say, "By God, I wasn't ready to die."

He was shunned by his neighbors. Once a drunk tried to kill him, but he survived the attempt. Although the identity of the man was known, no charges were filed. Finally, Rose had enough and moved to Louisiana.

Gradually, Rose was forgotten, and after many years had passed, historians weren't sure he even had existed. Then, in 1939, a researcher uncovered records showing that Rose had indeed lived. He had been a witness in several hearings involving people trying to claim state land as survivors of men killed at the Alamo.

One other story about Rose later grew up. It was said that when he died in Louisiana, a bed of yucca cacti grew out of his grave—growing from remnants of the thorns that pierced him when he fled from the Alamo. Since cactus thorns are not seeds, this—unlike the line in the sand—is clearly a legend.

outside. He made his way east on foot and after several days stopped at the farm of W. P. Zuber near Washington-on-the-Brazos. While he rested, he poured out the story to Zuber and his wife, who made him retell it over and over in his broken English. It wasn't until thirty-seven years later that the Zubers' son, having heard the story many times from his parents, wrote it all down.

On Friday, March 4, the Mexican battery to the north had been moved to within two hundred yards. Throughout the day, it pounded the north wall of the Alamo, the wall that had been broken during the battle in December and mended by the Texans with timber and dirt. The Mexicans knew this was the weakest spot.

Travis was doing what he could to prepare for the final assault. Inside the plaza, ditches were dug to which the men could retreat if the walls were taken. Inside the rooms along the west wall, rude shields were put up made of wooden poles and cowhide reinforced with dirt.

At 4 P.M. Santa Anna called a meeting of his senior officers. He asked them if the time was right for an attack. Some, like Ramírez y Sesma and Almonte, were eager, but others—among them Cós, who knew the Alamo only too well—weren't so sure. General Manuel Castrillón urged that they wait two more days for the twelve-pounder cannons, which could blast large holes in the Alamo's weakened walls. Other officers kept quiet. They knew, wrote Lieutenant Colonel José de la Peña, "that he [Santa Anna] would not tolerate opposition, his sole pleasure being in hearing what met with his wishes, while discarding all admonitions [warnings] that deviated from those wishes."[43]

The meeting broke up without a decision having been announced, but Santa Anna had already made up his mind to launch an attack on Sunday. Some historians have argued that he resented General Urrea's success against the Matamoros expedition and that he sought the glory of a bloody assault of the walls rather than standing off and battering the Alamo to pieces with heavy artillery. On the other hand, his own men were growing weary of the siege. Also, he may have reasoned that if the volunteers from Gonzales had come,

Santa Anna decided to have his troops scale the walls of the Alamo in an attack, rather than waiting for larger cannons to continue a siege of the building.

others might not be far behind, perhaps even Fannin.

The Mexican Plan

Santa Anna had spent that previous night and most of the next morning planning the assault and dictating the orders to a secretary. At 2 P.M., as Mexican batteries fired away, he announced to his staff that the attack would take place at 5 A.M. the following morning, March 6. The plan was simple: four columns would strike the Alamo at once with the heaviest blows against the vulnerable north wall. The first column, 400 men commanded by Cós, despite his promise to the Texans in December, would hit the northwest corner. The second, 380 men with Colonel Francisco Duque in command, would take the northeast corner. The third column, 400 men under Colonel José María Romero, would head for the east wall, and the fourth, 105 men led by Colonel Juan Morales, would come in from the south.

Ramírez y Sesma's cavalry would cover the east to round up any Texans who might try to get away. Santa Anna himself would command the reserves, which would be stationed to the north, where the signal to attack would be given.

Santa Anna was not one to plan a grand strategy and let underlings do the rest; he wanted to take care of everything himself. The orders specified that the troops should be in position by midnight. All should be wearing shoes or sandals; none would have a blanket or overcoat that might slow him down. Each column was as-signed an exact number of axes, crowbars, and ladders with which to climb the walls. Some companies were allotted six packages of cartridges per man; others, two. All bayonets should be sharpened. The orders concluded on a more poetic note:

> The honor of the nation being interested in this engagement against the bold and lawless foreigners who are occupying us, His Excellency [Santa Anna] expects that every man will do his duty, and exert himself to give a day of glory to the country, and of gratification to the Supreme Government, who will know how to reward the distinguished deeds of the brave soldiers of the army of Operations.[44]

Preparing for Attack

At 5 P.M. on March 5 the Mexican cannons, which had been firing almost nonstop all day, began to quiet. By 10 P.M. they were silent. Santa Anna wanted his troops to have an opportunity for sleep. Also, unlike the previous eleven nights, he wanted the Texans to sleep. He knew they must be exhausted and wanted them groggy and half-awake when Mexican soldiers began climbing the walls.

It must have been difficult, at least at first, for the men in the Alamo to sleep. They had seen the Mexicans preparing ladders and knew an attack would come any day. Some drew up simple wills. One, Dolphin Floyd, probably remembered that the next day was his twenty-first birthday.

Travis was not ready for rest. Since it was a cloudy, moonless night, he decided to send out one more messenger, sixteen-year-old Jim Allen. Allen led his horse out the

Although the situation was almost hopeless, Travis made one last appeal for aid the night before the Mexican attack.

Flags of the Alamo

There was no Texas flag during its fight for independence from Mexico. Instead, several flags were used, designed at various times for various components of the army.

The flag traditionally associated with the Alamo was much like that of Mexico, with vertical bands of green, white, and red. Instead of the Mexican eagle in the middle of the white band, however, was the date 1824. This was a reference to the Mexican constitution of 1824, which Santa Anna had nullified.

There is no proof that the 1824 flag ever flew over the Alamo, but three more flags were known to have been there. William Barret Travis had purchased a flag, but there is no record of what it looked like. The other two flags belonged to the First and Second Companies of New Orleans Greys, volunteer companies who joined the Texas army at the Battle of San Antonio.

Mexican accounts of the Battle of the Alamo describe how two young Mexican officers were killed in capturing an enemy flag but do not describe the flag. It was probably the blue silk flag of the First New Orleans Greys, which Santa Anna sent back to Mexico City after the battle. That flag remains on display in a museum there despite many attempts over the last hundred years to recover it. The 1824 flag could have been captured, as well, but Santa Anna would not have wanted to send to his capital any reminder of the constitution.

Other flags used by the Texans during the revolution included the "Come and Take It" banner at Gonzales, one made by a young Georgia woman that wound up at Goliad, and one featuring a half-nude goddess of liberty that was used at the Battle of San Jacinto. At least four flags featured a single star, including the one that eventually became the flag of the Republic of Texas and the State of Texas and resulted in the nickname "Lone Star State."

The flag of the First New Orleans Greys, captured at the Alamo by a Mexican officer.

gate and rode bareback through the night. Travis walked the walls, talking to the men on guard duty. He went into the chapel, the strongest part of the Alamo, where Susannah Dickinson, her daughter, and the rest of the women were sheltered and in which lay the often unconscious Bowie. He took off his gold ring with a black cat's-eye stone and tied a string through it. He hung the string around the neck of little Angelina Dickinson and said, "I won't have any more use for this. Keep it for me."[45]

Finally, even Travis gave in to weariness. He went to his quarters near the north wall and wrapped himself in a blanket. His sword and a shotgun were by his side. Near him was his servant Joe with a rifle.

"The Alamo Must Fall"

Outside the walls, the Mexican soldiers were finding it equally hard to sleep. De la Peña thought to himself that many of the men around him would, within a few hours, "be unable to answer questions addressed to us, having already returned to the nothingness whence we had come."[46] A soldier later wrote that "we remained flat on our stomachs until 5:30. *Caramba* [whew], it was cold."[47]

Santa Anna did not sleep. He was irritable through the long night, even threatening to stab his cook, Ben, with a sword if he didn't serve coffee faster. At one point, General Castrillón tried one last time to get him to postpone the attack and save Mexican lives. Santa Anna held up a partially eaten chicken leg. "What are the lives of soldiers more than so many chickens," he said. "I tell you, the Alamo must fall, and my orders must be obeyed at all hazards."[48]

As 5 A.M. neared, Santa Anna joined the reserve troops near the northern battery. Looking at him nervously was young José María Gonzales, a bugler from the *Zapadores* battalion. Santa Anna waited for what seemed an eternity. At last, he nodded to Gonzales, who blew the bugle call meaning "attention." More than fifteen hundred Mexican soldiers got to their feet. Shortly came a second bugle call, the one for "attack." Buglers from other companies echoed Gonzales's call, and the rush toward the Alamo began.

One of the Texans on duty who had managed to stay awake was John Baugh. He heard the bugle calls, but did not know what they meant. Then he heard a sound something like distant thunder that he realized was thousands of running feet. Turning toward the interior of the Alamo plaza, he bellowed, "The Mexicans are coming."[49]

Chapter

5 The Assault

For twelve days the Mexican army had besieged the Alamo. The Texans had waited, both for the attack they knew would come and the reinforcements they prayed would come. Santa Anna had waited, too, building his strength until the right moment. Now, after twelve days, the moment had arrived. Ninety minutes later, the Battle of the Alamo was over.

John Baugh's cry of alarm and the sound of Mexican bugles roused the Texans. They were not caught completely off guard. Most had been sleeping at their posts, three or four loaded muskets or rifles

Mexican troops attack the Alamo, ending the twelve-day siege.

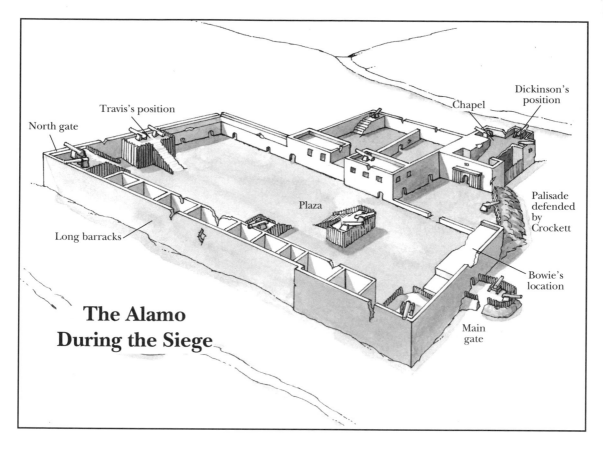

The Alamo During the Siege

North gate

Travis's position

Chapel

Dickinson's position

Palisade defended by Crockett

Long barracks

Plaza

Bowie's location

Main gate

at their side. The gunners also were close to their cannons, ready to fire at a moment's notice. Those few who had been inside grabbed their weapons and scampered up the dirt ramps leading to the top of the walls. They peered into the darkness, searching for targets, hearing the approaching Mexicans but unable to see them.

Then, the men of the second column (Duque's) were unable to contain their excitement. "*Viva la republica!*" they shouted. "*Viva Santa Anna!*" This enthusiasm, wrote de la Peña, "was paid for dearly."[50] The Texans on the east end of the north wall swung their eight-pounder toward the shouting and fired rounds of grapeshot and scrap metal. The effect was devastating. Half of one company—about forty men—were

killed or wounded with one blast. Another shot found the front of the column and wounded Duque, who fell and was trampled to death by his own men.

The Mexicans began to fire their muskets, even though many were still out of range. Mexican infantry (foot soldiers) were not taught to aim, but only to shoot directly forward. The sheer number of musket balls fired from a mass of men, the theory went, would make up for any lack of marksmanship. The trouble during the charge at the Alamo was that the Mexicans, firing on the run and from the hip, frequently shot far too high or—worse— shot too low. "Some of our men suffered the pain of falling from shots fired by their comrades,"[51] de la Peña wrote.

Muskets and Rifles

One traditional view of the Battle of the Alamo is that the Texans were sharp-shooting frontiersmen, picking off enemies at phenomenal range with hunting rifles, while the Mexicans were armed with primitive muskets. The truth is that, while both sides had some rifles, most of the men wielded muskets.

Certainly, muskets were inferior weapons. The inside of the barrels, or bores, of rifles contained spiral grooves called "rifling." These caused the balls or bullets to spin when fired, giving them far greater range and accuracy than those fired from muskets, which had smooth bores. At the time of the Battle of the Alamo, rifles could be effective up to about 300 yards and were accurate at 150 yards. Muskets had about half the range of rifles.

Probably, most of the men at the Alamo on both sides carried the British-made Tower musket, nicknamed the "Brown Bess." It was the primary weapon of the Mexican army, and since so many had been captured by the Texans in the early battles of the revolution, it is likely that many of the Alamo defenders carried it.

The volunteer companies who came to the Alamo from the United States were probably equipped with the U.S. Model 1816 musket. It was slightly smaller in caliber (the diameter of the barrel) than the Brown Bess, but the range was about the same.

The rifle in use by the Mexican army in 1836 was the British Baker, one of the first purely military rifles that could be fitted with a bayonet. Rifles used by the Texans were a hodgepodge of hunting rifles made by various manufacturers in the United States. The accuracy of these weapons, especially in the hands of veteran hunters such as David Crockett's "Tennessee Boys," was legendary, even among the Mexicans.

Rifles and muskets were fired in essentially the same way. A paper cartridge contained a charge of powder and a ball or bullet. The soldier would bite off the end of the cartridge containing the powder, pour a little in the priming pan, and pour the rest down the barrel, followed by the ball and the paper. Then, a ramrod would be used to pack powder and ball tightly together, held in place by the paper.

The rifle or musket would then be raised to the shoulder, aimed, and fired. Pressing the trigger released a hammer holding a piece of flint. The flint would strike a spark, igniting the powder in the priming pan, which in turn would ignite the powder in the barrel, firing the shot. Under ideal conditions, a musket or rifle could be fired about twice a minute.

A few of the Mexicans' shots, however, found their mark. Travis had been asleep when the alarm was sounded. He grabbed his sword and shotgun and, followed by Joe, who carried his own musket, Travis raced up the ramp to the top of the north wall and yelled, "Come on boys! The Mexicans are upon us, and we'll give them Hell!"[52]

The Death of Travis

A few of the Mexicans had reached the shelter of the wall, where they were safe from cannon fire but not from pistols, rifles, or muskets. To shoot at the men beneath their walls, however, the Texans had to lean over, exposing themselves to enemy fire. Just as Travis fired his shotgun at the soldiers below, a ball hit him in the forehead. He rolled back down the dirt ramp and came to rest with his back against a cannon, fatally wounded.

The Texans' cannons had been busy. The Mexican troops, dozens of their fellows dead and wounded, slowed and then began to retreat out of range. These men, however, were the cream of the Mexican army. Santa Anna had given instructions that only veteran troops were to be used in the attack. They quickly were re-formed by their officers and charged once more. This time, they were urged on by Santa Anna's band playing the *Degüello* (cutthroat), an eerie march dating from earlier centuries when the Arabic Moors occupied much of Spain. It signified that no mercy was to be shown, that every enemy must die. The music, de la Peña wrote, "inspired us to scorn life and to embrace death."[53]

The second charge met the same fate as the first. By now, the Texans probably had lit fires inside the Alamo plaza so that they could see to reload their weapons. In the glow, they could also see the advancing enemy. Bits of metal fired by their cannons mowed down the Mexicans. Sharpshooters were making every shot count. The attack wavered and fell back once more.

Showing exceptional bravery, the Mexicans gathered themselves for a third charge. Again, many fell before the hail of lead directed at them from the walls. This time, however, there was a difference. The first column, hit hard from the right, veered to the east instead of retreating. The third column, the one coming from the east, was hit from the left and turned to the west. The result was that all three columns rushed toward the north wall and succeeded in reaching it, forming, as de la Peña wrote, "a confused mass."[54]

Santa Anna, watching from his position to the north, was afraid the entire attack was collapsing. He ordered the reserves, and even his staff officers, to charge into the battle.

The Mexicans began to climb the walls. Only a few of the ladders had made it that far and some of them proved to be unable to carry a man's weight, but the attackers found a spot midway in the north wall that had been repaired with stones and timber—a surface rough enough to climb. The top of the wall was only two and a half feet wide. The first Mexicans to reach it did not have enough time to get their footing before they were shot or stabbed by the Texans.

The Mexicans kept climbing. De la Peña wrote that "the courage of our soldiers was not diminished as they saw their comrades falling dead or wounded, and they hurried to occupy their places and to avenge them, climbing over their bleeding bodies."[55] In the end there were too few Texans to keep them out. Led by General Juan Amador, a handful of Mexicans gained the top of the wall and engaged the Texans in hand-to-hand fighting, giving their comrades a chance to climb up.

At about the same time, Cós led his men back around to the northwest corner, where holes had been made in the wall through which cannons could be fired.

The Mexicans began firing into the Alamo through these holes and then wriggling through. Others threw ladders against the wall and started to climb. Again, they were too many and the Texans too few. Within minutes, the Mexicans were coming over the north wall in waves.

Colonel Morales, commanding the fourth column attacking from the south, had no more luck at first than the rest of

As flames leap through the windows of the Alamo, Mexican soldiers haul ladders to scale the walls.

Mexican soldiers stream over the walls of the Alamo during their attack. It would take a mere ninety minutes for the Mexicans to defeat the vastly outnumbered Texans.

the Mexicans. His troops ran into lethal fire from Crockett and his Tennesseans as well as from the cannons by the main gate and those along the stockade fence Crockett defended. The Mexicans moved to their left, seeking shelter among some of the burned-out huts in La Villita. From there, they sprinted to the southeast corner of the Alamo, scaled a platform on which the eighteen-pounder was mounted, and killed the Texans manning it. Dropping down into the plaza, they charged the main gate from behind, killed the defenders there, and opened the gate at about the same time as the Mexicans came over the north wall.

Now, it was only a matter of time. The Texans, forced from the walls, retreated wherever they could. Some were trapped in the middle of the plaza and cut down. Others sought any shelter that was available. Sixteen-year-old Galba Fuqua ran into the

Mexican soldiers and Texans square off in hand-to-hand combat after the Mexicans enter the Alamo. The Mexicans were under orders to take no prisoners.

chapel sacristy (a small room where items for religious services were normally stored) where Susannah Dickinson held her baby daughter. Fuqua had been shot in the jaw. He tried to speak, holding his jaw together, but could get no words out. He turned and ran back to the fighting.

Many of the Texans raced into the barracks on the east and west sides of the plaza. There, they took shelter behind their cowhide and dirt shields and fired at the Mexicans through small holes in the walls. The Mexicans, directed by General Amador, wheeled the Texans' cannons up to each room, blasted through the doors, fired a volley, then rushed in with bayonets. In their excitement, some of the Mexicans, wrote de la Peña, "blind with fury and smoke, fired their shots against friends and enemies alike, and in this way our losses were most grievous."[56]

Some of the defenders tried to surrender, even using white stockings on the end of bayonets as a sign. De la Peña wrote that when the Mexicans entered the room after such a signal

> those among the enemy . . . who had no thought of surrendering . . . would meet them with pistol shots and bayonets. Thus betrayed, our men rekindled their anger and at every moment fresh skirmishes broke out with renewed fury.[57]

A Heroic Act

A group of young Mexican officers spotted an enemy flag atop the barracks. Traditionally, the flag flown by the Texans over the Alamo was a version of the red, white, and green Mexican flag with the date 1824, symbolizing the constitution Santa Anna had abandoned. There is no evidence it was flying on March 6. What the Mexicans saw was the silk banner of the New Orleans Greys. Lieutenant José María Torres ran toward the flag and ripped it down. As he tried to raise the Mexican flag, he was wounded. Lieutenant Damasco Martínez ran to help him. Together, they raised the flag of Mexico above the Alamo, although both were killed in the attempt.

Some of the Texans tried to escape from the Alamo altogether. At least five were observed climbing over the east wall. Most were easy prey for Ramírez y Sesma's cavalry. One managed to hide under a bridge. The next day, discovered by a local woman doing her laundry in the river, he was arrested and shot. Only one of the Alamo's defenders got away. Henry Warnell, although badly hurt, made his way to freedom only to die of his wounds three months later.

The slaughter continued. Bowie's sisters-in-law, Juana Alsbury and Gertrudis Navarro, huddled together in a room on the west wall. Navarro courageously opened the door, pleading with the Mexicans not to shoot into their room. Soldiers tore her shawl from her shoulders, and she fell back against the wall. Her sister Juana held her one-year-old son, "supposing he would be motherless soon."[58] Edwin Mitchell, a wounded Texan who had taken refuge in the room, rose up to defend the women and, as Juana wrote, "the soldiers bayoneted him at my side."[59]

Breaking into a room on the south wall near the main gate, Mexican soldiers found Jim Bowie so ill he could barely raise the pistols given to him earlier by Crockett. Even as he fired, his body was pierced by musket balls and bayonets. He probably never had a chance to use his famous knife, although later stories claimed he killed several Mexicans with it before he died. Later, a Mexican soldier who obviously did not know about Bowie's illness wrote that he "died like a woman, hidden almost under a mattress."[60]

Almeron Dickinson was in charge of the three twelve-pounders at the east end of the roofless chapel, the strongest part of the Alamo. From there, he had seen Morales's men succeed in entering through the south wall of the plaza. He ran down the dirt ramp into the sacristy and shouted to his wife, "Great God, Sue, the Mexicans are inside the walls. If they spare you, save my child."[61] He gave her a quick embrace, then raced back to his guns.

He and his men swung their cannons around and fired at the Mexicans streaming through the south gate, killing dozens. As in the plaza, however, the Texans' own cannon was used against them. Morales ordered the huge eighteen-pounder swung around so that it could be fired at the platform inside the chapel. In moments, the Texans were dead—among them Dickinson, Bonham, and a *Tejano* named Gregorio Esparza, whose eight-year-old son, Enrique, was huddled below with his mother and baby sister.

Slaughter in the Chapel

The chapel's guns had been silenced, but some defenders remained inside. The eighteen-pounder was then trained on the thick, oak doors, which soon splintered and crashed inward. Mexican soldiers rushed into the chapel, firing wildly. Many years later, Enrique Esparza remembered:

They swarmed among us and over us. They fired on us in vollies. They struck us down with their *escopetas* [muskets]. In the dark our men groped and

Señora Candelaria

There are different versions of how the death of James Bowie occurred. The most detailed and colorful came from a person who claimed to have been an eyewitness, but there is reason to doubt her story.

One of the survivors of the Battle of the Alamo was a *Tejano* woman of San Antonio named Andrea Castañon Ramírez Villanueva, nicknamed Señora Candelaria after a local, waxy shrub sometimes used to make candles. Señora Candelaria was a *curandero*, a Mexican folk healer who used herbs and other remedies together with prayers, chants, and lighted candles in order to cure disease. As an old woman, she would entertain visitors with tales of the Alamo.

She claimed to have received a personal letter from General Sam Houston asking her to "take care of Bowie, my brother." She said she slipped past Mexican soldiers into the Alamo and was placed in charge of the ill Bowie.

Toward the end of the battle, she later said,

> I had hard work keeping Colonel Bowie on his couch. He got hold of his two pistols and began firing them off, shouting all the while to his men not to give up. . . . Finally a bullet whizzed through the door, grazing my chin—see, it left a scar which is still there today—and killed Bowie. I had the Colonel in my arms.

While it is possible Bowie died this way, other parts of Señora Candelaria's story raise the suspicion that most of it was her invention. She claimed, for instance, that "Davy Crockett died fighting like a wild beast" and that "brave Colonel Travis within a few feet the other way." In fact, Crockett evidently was killed after the battle and, at any rate, was at the far south end of the Alamo while Travis fell at the north wall.

Another Alamo survivor, Susannah Dickinson, did not mention Señora Candelaria at all in her account of the battle. In fact, when Señora Candelaria's stories began to spread, Mrs. Dickinson called her a fraud. Most people, however, seemed to believe her, and she even received a small pension from the state of Texas. She died in 1899, claiming to be 114 years old.

Señora Candelaria

Texas defenders fire on their Mexican attackers. Virtually uncontrollable in the heat of battle, the Mexicans even slaughtered patients in the makeshift hospital.

grasped the throats of our foemen and buried their knives into their hearts. . . . By my side was an American boy. He was about my age but larger. . . . As they rushed upon him he stood calmly and across his shoulders drew the blanket on which he had slept. He was unarmed. They slew him where he stood and his corpse fell over me.[62]

The slain boy was one of two sons of Antony Wolfe, who was fighting inside the chapel. Seeing one of his sons killed, Wolfe picked up the other boy in his arms and raced up the dirt ramp to the platform where the dead Texan gunners lay. In desperation, wrote de la Peña, he "was seen to hurl himself from a considerable height, both perishing in the same blow."[63]

Robert Evans tried to take as many of the Mexicans as possible with him. He ran toward a room just off the chapel where several hundred pounds of gunpowder were stored. He carried a flaming torch, intending to blow up the chapel and everyone in it. He was shot down only a few feet from his goal.

In the tiny sacristy Susannah Dickinson crouched in a corner, holding her daughter, Angelina. Jacob Walker, a young man from Gonzales whom Susannah Dickinson knew well, ran into the room, looking for a place to hide. Four Mexicans ran in after him, stabbed him with their bayonets, and then "lifted him up like a farmer does a bundle of fodder on a pitchfork,"[64] raising and lowering him several times before he finally died. More Mexicans stormed into the sacristy, muskets blazing. Mrs. Dickinson was slightly wounded in the leg before an officer got control of his men.

Walker was probably the last man killed in the actual fighting, but the Mexicans were, in Mrs. Dickinson's words, "drunk on blood."[65] They broke into the room that had been used as a hospital, slaughtering the sick and wounded. They raced around the Alamo, shooting into the bodies of

Texans, stabbing them with bayonets. They even cornered a stray cat and killed it, yelling, "It is not a cat, but an American."[66]

Finally, at about 6:30 A.M., the firing stopped and the smoke began to clear. Santa Anna, who had taken no part in the fighting, walked into the Alamo, picking his way among the bodies of his men and the bodies of those who had so stubbornly resisted him. De la Peña wrote:

> He could see for himself the desolation among his battalions and that devastated area littered with corpses, with scattered limbs and bullets, with weapons and torn uniforms. Some of these were burning together with the corpses, which produced an unbearable and nauseating odor. The bodies, with their blackened and bloody faces disfigured by a desperate death,

Susannah Dickinson was shot in the leg during the attack on the Alamo, though she would be one of the few to survive the battle.

their hair and uniforms burning at once, presented a dreadful and truly hellish sight.[67]

The Death of Crockett

Miraculously, a half-dozen Texans had escaped the slaughter and were discovered hiding in a back room. Mexican soldiers rushed forward to kill them, but General Castrillón intervened. He placed his hand on his heart, saying, "Here is a hand and a heart to protect you; come with me to the General-in-Chief [Santa Anna] and you shall be saved."[68]

Castrillón led his prisoners through the smoke, fire, and corpses to where Santa Anna was standing, surrounded by his personal staff. Colonel Fernando Urizza reported that Castrillón led "a venerable-looking old man by the hand."[69] Urizza and de la Peña, both of whom were witnesses, wrote that the old man was none other than Crockett. According to de la Peña, who called him a "naturalist,"[70] Crockett claimed he had been exploring the territory and just happened to find himself in San Antonio when the Mexican army arrived.

"Santa Anna, the august," Castrillón said, "I deliver up to you six brave prisoners of war." Santa Anna was furious. He had given instructions that there was to be no mercy. The *Degüello* had been played. "Who has given you orders to take prisoners?" he demanded of Castrillón. "I do not want to see those men living. Shoot them!"[71]

Most of his officers were shocked. They stood silently, none venturing to give the order. But some of Santa Anna's personal aides, who had remained with him through the battle, were eager to please

A drawing depicts Davy Crockett being killed while bravely fighting his Mexican attackers. Mexican eyewitnesses, however, say that Crockett was killed after having been taken prisoner.

their chief and be able to say they had contributed to the victory. They drew their swords and, wrote de la Peña,

> fell upon these unfortunate, defenseless men just as a tiger leaps upon his prey. Though tortured before they were killed, these unfortunates died without complaining and without humiliating themselves before their torturers. . . . I turned away horrified in order not to witness such a barbarous scene.[72]

The legend was to grow later that Crockett had died fighting, swinging Old Betsy like a club after he ran out of ammunition. Other stories claimed he was not killed at all, but was taken prisoner to Mexico where he lived out his years in the silver mines. The Mexican witnesses, however, had no reason to tell anything but the truth. At least it can be said that Crockett, even if he didn't die fighting, died bravely.

With the deaths of Crockett and his comrades, the Battle of the Alamo came to an end. Later that morning, Santa Anna pointed to the bodies and said to Colonel Urizza, "These are the chickens. Much blood has been shed; but the battle is over. It was but a small affair."[73] He did not realize until weeks later how much the "small affair" would contribute to his ultimate defeat.

6 The Aftermath

Late on the afternoon of the fall of the Alamo, the bodies of the defenders were stacked between layers of dry wood and set on fire. It must have seemed to Texas that its revolution had gone up in flames, as well. The government, the army, and the civilian population panicked, retreating headlong to the east. Santa Anna, however, was confident that his victory would be complete in only a few weeks. The end would come soon, but not as the Mexican president planned.

After the killing stopped, Santa Anna ordered the survivors brought before him. There were only a handful—Susannah Dickinson and her daughter, Bowie's

A painting depicts survivors of the Battle of the Alamo pleading for their lives in front of the victorious Mexican army.

sisters-in-law, Travis's servant Joe, the Esparza family, and a few other women and children. Santa Anna had demonstrated his lack of pity; now, it was time to show his generosity. He gave a blanket and two silver coins to each of the women and set them free. He questioned Mrs. Dickinson and was enraptured with little Angelina, offering to adopt her. Mrs. Dickinson begged to be allowed to keep her daughter, and when Colonel Almonte took her side, Santa Anna gave up the idea.

El presidente did, however, want Mrs. Dickinson to tell the rest of Texas the fate of the Alamo and the might of the Mexican army. To impress her, he organized a parade of troops that, only a few hours before, had been in battle. He sent his cook Ben, a black American, with her as a guide. He also wrote a message for her to carry, saying that "some exemplary punishment" had been dealt out to "a parcel of audacious adventurers."[74]

Meanwhile, there were the dead and wounded to deal with. Santa Anna gave the job of disposing of the bodies to Francisco Ruiz, the *alcalde* (mayor) of San Antonio. The Mexicans were to be buried in the Campo Santo cemetery; the Texans were to be cremated. At 5 P.M., the fire was lit. A teenage boy, Pablo Díaz, saw

> an immense pillar of flame shoot up a short distance to the south and east of the Alamo and the dense smoke from it rise high in the clouds. . . . I went to the place. The crowd was gathered around the smouldering embers and ashes of the fire. . . . I did not need to make an inquiry. The story was told by the silent witnesses before me. Fragments of flesh, bones and charred wood and ashes revealed it in all its terrible truth.[75]

The Lost Grave

A year later, Juan Seguin placed some of the ashes and bones in a coffin draped with the flag of the Republic of Texas. It was carried in a solemn procession into San Antonio and buried in a peach orchard. The site of the burial was not marked, and many years later people sought it in vain. Memorials exist, not only in San Antonio but also throughout Texas, honoring the defenders of the Alamo, but no one knows where their bones lie.

Historians continue to debate the numbers killed at the Alamo. In his victory message to Mexico City, Santa Anna claimed 606 Texans died, a wild exaggeration intended to make the battle seem larger than it actually was. De la Peña, Almonte, and Colonel José Navarro put the number at about 250. The most reliable count was by Ruiz, who wrote, "The men burnt numbered one hundred and eighty two. I was an eyewitness."[76]

The number of Mexican dead is even harder to pinpoint. Santa Anna, seeking to minimize his losses, claimed only 70 were killed and 370 wounded. About the same number was given by Almonte, de la Peña, and Navarro. On the other hand, Ruiz, in charge of the burial, wrote that "Santa Anna's loss was estimated at 1600 men."[77] Ruiz could not provide a more definite figure. The Mexicans were buried in mass graves, and when there was no more room in the cemetery, were thrown into the San Antonio River. The very fact that Ruiz ran out of space implies there were many more than 70 corpses.

In a way, the dead Mexicans were lucky. Santa Anna had neglected to bring adequate medical supplies and doctors.

The Fate of the Alamo

After the Battle of the Alamo, the Mexican army wanted to make sure the Texans could never again use it as a fort. Walls were knocked down with cannon fire or blown up with gunpowder. The cannons the Mexicans couldn't use themselves were dumped in the San Antonio River or down a well.

The Alamo stood, crumbling and empty, until 1842, when the Republic of Texas gave it to the Roman Catholic Church, which tried but was unable to make it a place of worship once more. In 1847, the church rented it to the U.S. Army, which wanted it as a supply depot. The army restored the chapel, putting on a new roof and adding the "hump" on the front that gives the Alamo its famous shape. The army also restored the Long Barracks, but the rest of the buildings disappeared and the area was built over.

During the Civil War, a militia unit, the Alamo City Guards, occupied the building, preparing it for possible invasion by Union troops. After the war, the Alamo was once more leased by the church to the U.S. Army as a supply depot.

When the army built a new supply depot in 1876 and no longer needed the Alamo, the church sold the Long Barracks to a merchant named Honoré Grenet, who built a large store around the older structure. Grenet rented the Alamo chapel from the church to be used as a warehouse.

It was not until 1883, almost a half-century after the battle, that the people of Texas gave a thought to preserving the Alamo. The state of Texas bought the chapel that year for $20,000, and two years later turned it over to the city of San Antonio.

In 1885, Grenet died and his store was sold to the Hugo & Schmeltzer Company, who ran it until 1903, when the company became interested in selling it to someone who wanted to turn it into a hotel. To prevent this, the Daughters of the Republic of Texas, a women's group that had been established in 1881 to preserve the history of the revolution, set out to raise $75,000 to buy the property. They were unsuccessful, but one of their wealthy members, twenty-three-year-old Clara Driscoll, bought the property herself and gave it to the state of Texas, which in turn entrusted it to the Daughters of the Republic of Texas, who have maintained it ever since.

Over the years, the chapel was restored and opened to the public, and a museum and library were built on the grounds. In 1936, the hundredth anniversary of the battle, the Long Barracks were restored to house a historical display. Today, the Alamo is one of the top tourist attractions in the United States, attracting about three million visitors each year.

De la Peña wrote:

> One could hardly enter the places erroneously called hospitals without trembling in horror. The wailing of the wounded and their just complaints penetrated the innermost recesses of the heart; there was no one to extract a bullet, no one to perform an amputation, and many unfortunates died whom medical science could have saved.[78]

Report of the Battle

The citizens of Gonzales had a good idea what had happened at the Alamo. They had not heard the boom of the eighteen-pounder, which Travis had said would be fired three times a day, since the morning of March 6. More than one hundred volunteers had congregated there, having come from throughout Texas in answer to Travis's pleas.

On March 11, General Sam Houston arrived in Gonzales to take command, still thinking he might be in time to relieve Travis. That afternoon, however, two *Tejanos* rode into town, reporting that the Alamo had fallen. Houston suspected they might be spies and arrested them, not wanting to start an unnecessary panic. On March 13 he sent his own hard-of-hearing scout, Erastus "Deaf" Smith, to discover the truth.

Smith had been gone only a few hours when he met Susannah Dickinson, Ben, and Travis's servant Joe, who had joined them. By midnight, Houston and the Texas army were in retreat, along with the population of Gonzales. Three cannons were dumped into the river to prevent the Mexicans from getting them, and the town was burned to the ground to deny the enemy any shelter.

The largest body of Texas troops—more than four hundred—remained in Goliad, and Houston sent orders to Fannin to blow up the *presidio* and retreat. But Fannin, as usual, was not a man to act either quickly or decisively. As General Urrea's troops drew closer, Fannin wavered between obeying Houston or making a stand. A young soldier, Herman Ehrenberg, later wrote that "it seemed that one plan after another passed through his [Fannin's] head. The large number seemed to confuse and to hinder him."[79] First, he decided to retreat and buried all his cannons. Then, he changed his mind and had them all dug up—then buried again—then dug up again.

By the time Fannin finally decided to leave, Urrea had reached Goliad. At 9 A.M. on March 19, the Texans took advantage of a thick fog to slip out of the *presidio* and head east. When it was discovered they were gone, they were already miles away, but instead of making haste, they creaked along, oxen pulling fully loaded wagons.

Urrea, in rapid pursuit, was determined to celebrate this day—his birthday—with a victory. Fannin reached an open area near Coleto Creek and halted. A forest was in sight, but Fannin couldn't make up his mind whether to stay where he was or head for the shelter of the trees. At last, the man who couldn't make up his mind had it made up for him. Urrea's swift cavalry swept past the Texans, trapping them in the meadow.

Fannin formed his troops into a square. All day, the two sides traded musket fire. Fannin was wounded in the thigh, but the Texans held on. The next morning, however, they found that the main

"Deaf" Smith

Erastus Smith was not at the Battle of the Alamo, but he was practically everywhere else during the Texas Revolution. Although not usually placed on the same heroic level as Travis, Bowie, Crockett, or Houston, Smith was perhaps more valuable than any of them.

He was born in 1787 in New York, but his father moved the family west and eventually settled in Mississippi. A childhood disease left him with weak lungs, a 70 percent hearing loss, and a nickname—"Deaf," usually pronounced "Deef."

Smith first came to Texas in 1817 with a filibustering expedition and settled permanently in San Antonio in 1821, finding the dry air good for his lungs. He became famous as a hunter and scout and probably knew Texas better than anyone else. He claimed that the outdoor life, including the eating of skunk meat, improved his health.

Although he married a *Tejano* widow, built a house in San Antonio, and had a large family, he never lost his taste for adventure. He was one of the men who accompanied Bowie in his search for the San Saba silver mine and survived the resulting Indian battle.

At first, he sympathized more with Mexico than with the Texians but was infuriated when General Cós threatened to put Texas under martial law in 1835. He volunteered to serve as a scout and was with Bowie at the Battle of Mission Concepción and with Ben Milam at the Battle of San Antonio.

He was one of only four men accompanying Houston to Gonzales in March of 1836 and was the person who found Susannah Dickinson as she made her way east from the Alamo. Before the Battle of San Jacinto, he went into the Mexican camp as a spy, pretending to be a deaf-mute laborer. Just before the battle, he was given the crucial task of cutting down the bridge over Vince's Bayou to prevent the Mexican army from escaping. Afterward, it was Smith who took a message from Santa Anna to the remaining Mexican generals, ordering them to return to Mexico.

After the war, Smith served in the Texas Rangers, fighting in many battles against Indians. His health soon failed, however, and he died in 1837. The grateful Republic of Texas gave his wife four thousand acres of land, a large house in San Antonio, and a generous (for that time) allowance of $500 a year.

Acting under orders from Santa Anna, Lieutenant Colonel José Portilla and his troops gun down the helpless prisoners captured at Goliad.

body of Urrea's troops had arrived, as well as several cannons. Surrounded, outgunned, outnumbered, with no water and little food, there was no choice but to surrender. Urrea said that the Texans must surrender unconditionally or be killed where they stood. Fannin had no choice. He signed the agreement, and the Texans were marched nine miles back to Goliad.

The Fate of the Prisoners

For more than a week, Urrea pondered what to do with all his prisoners—now more than five hundred, a group of New York volunteers having been captured as they landed on the coast. He was aware that Santa Anna had ordered that no prisoners be taken, but was hesitant to order Fannin and the rest killed. While on a mission to nearby Victoria he wrote to Santa Anna, recommending the Texans be put to work instead. Santa Anna wrote back, "I yield to no one, my friend, in tenderheartedness."[80] Santa Anna ordered that

the prisoners be executed immediately, sending the order personally to Lieutenant Colonel José Nicolás Portilla—in command in Urrea's absence. Portilla received the order from Santa Anna on the same day he received another one from Urrea to "treat the prisoners well, especially Fannin."[81] After spending a sleepless night, Portilla decided to obey Santa Anna.

On March 27—Palm Sunday—most of the Texans were formed into three groups and marched out of Goliad in different directions. Some thought they were on their way to the coast to be sent to the United States. Others, however, noticed that the Mexican soldiers guarding them were not equipped for a long march. A few miles outside the fort, they were halted, forced to kneel, and shot down. Only a few managed to escape.

Fannin and the rest of the wounded had been kept in Goliad. They were herded into an open area and told they were being taken to the coast. In the distance, however, they could hear gunfire and knew what was happening. A survivor later said that "some turned pale, but not one displayed the least fear or quivering."[82] Fannin gave his gold watch to Captain Carolino Huerta, asking in return that he not be shot in the head and that his body be buried. "With all the necessary formalities,"[83] Huerta replied. Fannin then was sat in a chair, blindfolded, and shot in the head at point-blank range by a firing squad at Huerta's command. His body was burned.

The rest of the wounded were shot or bayoneted. More than four hundred men had been butchered. The only ones spared were doctors, urgently needed to tend the Mexican wounded in San Antonio; skilled craftsmen such as carpenters; and the New Yorkers. Most of Santa Anna's army was shocked. De la Peña would write, "So many and such cold-blooded murders tarnished our glory, took away the fruits of victory."[84]

The Runaway Scrape

The news of the massacre at Goliad, coming on the heels of the fall of the Alamo, threw Texas into a panic. Colonists loaded their belongings onto carts and wagons and headed east. Herman Ehrenberg, who escaped the slaughter at Goliad, found farmhouses with food still on the table, chickens roosting in living rooms. Land speculator William Gray, who had been in Washington-on-the-Brazos for the convention, wrote that "thousands are moving off to the east. A constant stream of women and children, and some men . . . are rushing across the Brazos night and day."[85]

The people were afraid that Santa Anna was coming—and so he was. He moved out of San Antonio on March 31,

determined to deliver the final blow to the rebellion. His aides had told him that the war was all but over, that he ought to return to Mexico City and let his generals mop up, but his pride would not let him. Already, he was growing jealous of Urrea, who had captured both the Matamoros expedition and Goliad. No, he vowed, the final victory would belong to Santa Anna.

His army advanced on three fronts. He sent General Gaona northeast to the Colorado River, from which he was to cross to the Brazos and then head south. Urrea was to advance from the southwest, and Santa Anna would command the central thrust. It was this three-pronged advance that scattered the Texans before it.

Right along with the Texans went their brand-new government. Gray wrote that the delegates at Washington "are dispersing in all directions with haste and in confusion."[86] The new president, David Burnet, and his top officials headed for the coast. At one stop, Burnet was provided with a bed, but others had to sleep on the floor, the secretary of the navy and the attorney general of the new republic sharing a blanket.

The Texas army was moving east, too, slowly growing larger as more volunteers from the United States joined it, making up for the Texans who left Houston to see to the safety of their families. Houston saw that his army stayed well away from the Mexicans, who were marching from the west. His troops were ashamed of what they considered cowardice; they wanted to turn and fight. Texans later called Houston's retreat and the Texans' headlong flight the "Runaway Scrape."

The government of Texas also wanted a battle. "The enemy are laughing you to scorn," Burnet wrote to Houston. "You must fight them. You must retreat no

Houston

Sam Houston served Texas as commander of the army, president, senator, and governor. In the end, however, he died a lonely old man, rejected by his state.

Houston was born in 1793 in Virginia and moved to Tennessee in 1807 with his mother and eight brothers and sisters. Shortly afterward, he ran away from home and lived for a time with the Cherokee Indians, who called him "the Raven."

He returned to civilization and ran a school in 1812 before joining the army. He saw action in the War of 1812, mainly against the Creek Indians, who were allies of the British. He was severely wounded at the Battle of Horseshoe Bend, but his bravery caught the attention of General Andrew Jackson, who became his friend and supporter.

With Jackson's backing, Houston entered politics and was twice elected to the U.S. Congress before winning the governorship of Tennessee in 1827. He was even mentioned as a possible presidential candidate, but in 1829, Eliza Allen, Houston's bride of only four months, left him. No reason was ever revealed, but the rumors drove Houston from office.

Depressed, he went to Arkansas to live once more with the Cherokees. He became an alcoholic and soon was given another nickname, "Big Drunk." In 1832, he went to Washington, D.C., to visit Jackson, then president, on behalf of the Cherokees, who were in danger of being moved from their homeland. Jackson suggested that he go to Texas. It has generally been believed that Jackson sent Houston to Texas for the specific purpose of bringing it into the United States.

After the Texas Revolution, Houston was elected president of the Republic of Texas twice. After Texas became a state, Houston served as a U.S. senator from 1846 to 1859. He resigned from the Senate in 1859 and was elected governor of Texas, becoming the only man ever to be governor of two states.

Houston's downfall came when Texas voted to join the Confederate States of America shortly after the beginning of the Civil War. He believed Texas should remain in the United States, but most Texans, including even Houston's sons, were against him. When Texas voted to leave the United States in March 1861, Houston refused to sign the Ordinance of Secession and was removed as governor. He lived two more years before dying in obscurity in 1863. His last words were, "Texas. Texas."

farther. The country expects you to fight."[87] Another time, he wrote, "Have we so far forgotten our wonted boasts of Superior prowess as to turn our backs to an equal number of a foe that has given us every imaginable incentive to action?"[88]

Houston's Plan

Houston, however, might have been following a plan. Although it has never been proven, he was possibly trying to draw Santa Anna into a trap by bringing him closer to the United States, whose president, Andrew Jackson, wanted Texas badly. Jackson had been almost like a fa-

Sam Houston commanded the Texans during the Battle of San Jacinto. Both Santa Anna and Houston were eager for a fight.

ther to Houston, and may have sent him to Texas for the deliberate purpose of snatching Texas from Mexico. Jackson had sent General Edmund Gaines to western Louisiana, perhaps hoping that Santa Anna could be lured east of the Sabine River into the old Neutral Ground, where Gaines would have an excuse for attacking him. While Gaines waited, he kept in touch with Houston. It was no accident that about two hundred of Gaines's troops "deserted" and joined Houston in Texas.

Gaines, however, never found an excuse to cross into Texas. At San Felipe, Houston turned his army north. When Santa Anna arrived at San Felipe, he turned south toward Harrisburg (now the city of Houston), hoping to catch the fleeing Texas government. Houston faced a decision. If he continued toward Louisiana, Santa Anna might eventually follow him, but the Texas army might completely lose faith and desert. On April 16, the Texas army came to a fork in the road. Nacogdoches and Louisiana were to the left; Harrisburg, to the right. As Houston swung his horse toward Harrisburg, his men cheered.

Houston had received information that Santa Anna, in his effort to catch the government, had ridden ahead of his army with 750 cavalry, about the same number of troops Houston had. If Houston could manage to catch and trap Santa Anna into a battle, he would have a chance for a victory.

Santa Anna reached Harrisburg on April 15 and learned that Burnet and the rest of the Texas cabinet had fled east to New Washington. He also was told that Houston and his army were about fifty miles to the north. Almonte was sent racing ahead with a company of troops to capture the Texas officials but arrived just as they were rowing away from the shore toward a ship that would take them to Galveston. They were in musket range, but Almonte ordered his men not to fire since Burnet's wife was in the boat.

Enraged, Santa Anna decided to resume his pursuit of Houston, not realizing that Houston was pursuing him. He reached New Washington on April 18 and received word that Houston had reached Harrisburg and was again retreating, this time toward Lynch's Ferry across the San Jacinto River. Santa Anna was determined to reach the ferry first and cut the Texans off.

Ready for Battle

Houston, however, reached Lynch's Ferry first, but he intended to fight, not flee. Marching all night, the Texans crossed a wooden bridge over Vince's Bayou on the morning of April 20 and found themselves on a small plain almost entirely surrounded by rivers, bayous, and swamps. Houston headed north to Lynch's Ferry, but instead of crossing, drew his army up in a defensive position in the trees.

Santa Anna arrived that afternoon to find Houston facing him. He ordered his army to halt and put his troops in battle formation. Throughout the afternoon, the armies probed at one another, sending groups of cavalrymen into small skirmishes and firing their cannons. The Mexicans had only a single nine-pounder, and the Texans had two six-pounders, the "Twin Sisters," a gift from the people of Cincinnati, Ohio.

Night came, but there was little sleep in the Mexican camp. Santa Anna realized

he was in a bad position and sent a rider to General Cós a few miles back, urging him to bring his five hundred men on the run. He expected that Houston would attack that night, before any Mexican reinforcements had a chance to arrive, and had his troops on alert. Dawn came, however, and the Texas camp was quiet.

The morning wore on. At 9 A.M. Cós's troops arrived, but they were mostly recruits rather than veterans. Too many veterans had fallen at the Alamo. Still, the Mexicans now outnumbered their enemy by about five hundred. Noon came and went with no sign of attack. Finally, Santa Anna ordered his weary men to stack their weapons and rest. He retired to his tent and is supposed to have dallied there with a mulatto (a person of mixed race) named Emily Morgan—called the "Yellow Rose of Texas" because of her skin color—who was actually a spy sent by Houston.

Not only the Mexicans, but also the Texans wondered what Houston was thinking. His men were furious that he had done nothing to prevent Cós from arriving. Colonel John Wharton went through the camp, saying, "Boys, there is no other word to-day, but fight, fight!"[89] At last, about 3:30 P.M., Houston began to form his troops into a battle line. They moved silently through the tall grass, accompanied by a piper and drummer playing a popular ballad of the day that went, "Won't you come to the bower I have shaded for you?"[90]

The Battle of San Jacinto

As the Texans drew closer to the Mexican camp, Deaf Smith rode up, waving an ax. On Houston's orders, he had cut down the bridge over Vince's Bayou. No more Mexicans would be able to reach Santa Anna. On the other hand, there was no way for the Texans to retreat. It was to be an all-or-nothing battle. Incredibly, the Mexicans had no advance guard to warn them of the Texans' approach. When they were two hundred yards from Santa Anna's camp, Houston ordered the Twin Sisters into action. "Now is the critical time," he shouted. "Fire away!"[91]

The cannons roared, and missiles of scrap iron sprayed the Mexican camp, killing many while they slept. The Texans fired a volley with their muskets and rifles, then charged. Colonel Sidney Sherman, commanding a cavalry regiment, shouted, "Remember the Alamo!" Immediately, the battle cry was taken up by most of the army, many adding, "Remember Goliad!"

Before most of the Mexicans could rouse themselves from sleep and get their weapons, the Texans were upon them—shooting, clubbing, slashing with Bowie knives, and screaming all the while, "Remember the Alamo!" A bugler tried to alert the camp and was shot dead in mid-note. Some of the officers tried to rally their men, but it was too late. The shattered Mexican army broke and ran. The Battle of San Jacinto was over. It had lasted eighteen minutes.

The killing, unfortunately, went on much longer. Most of the Texans had lost family members or friends in the Alamo or at Goliad. They were out for blood. Unarmed Mexicans knelt and cried, "Me no Alamo!" only to be massacred without mercy. Houston tried to stop his men, but they ignored him. Finally, he said, "Gentle-

During the Battle of San Jacinto the Texans continued to slaughter the Mexicans, even after their surrender. Although Houston tried to stop them, the Texans eagerly sought revenge for the deaths of friends and relatives at the Alamo and at Goliad.

men, I applaud your bravery but damn your manners,"[92] and rode off. The butchery did not stop until dark. More than 650 Mexicans had been killed. About 700 survived to become prisoners. The Texan casualties were 8 killed and 18 wounded, including Houston, who had been hit in the ankle.

Santa Anna had not been among the Mexicans who tried to make a stand. Instead, he had leaped on a horse and fled. Unable to cross Vince's Bayou, he spent the night hiding in bushes, having somehow changed into the uniform of an ordinary private. The next morning, he was captured and led back to where other prisoners were being kept. When he arrived, the Mexicans stood and shouted, *"El presidente! El presidente!"*

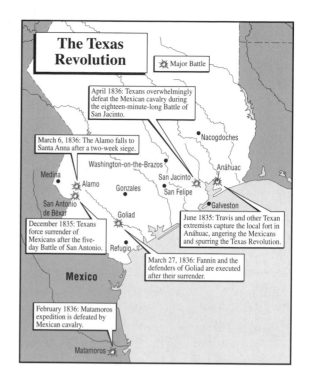

The Texas Revolution

Major Battle

April 1836: Texans overwhelmingly defeat the Mexican cavalry during the eighteen-minute-long Battle of San Jacinto.

March 6, 1836: The Alamo falls to Santa Anna after a two-week siege.

June 1835: Travis and other Texan extremists capture the local fort in Anáhuac, angering the Mexicans and spurring the Texas Revolution.

December 1835: Texans force surrender of Mexicans after the five-day Battle of San Antonio.

March 27, 1836: Fannin and the defenders of Goliad are executed after their surrender.

February 1836: Matamoros expedition is defeated by Mexican cavalry.

Nacogdoches

Washington-on-the-Brazos

Medina

Alamo

Gonzales

San Jacinto

Anáhuac

San Antonio de Béxar

Goliad

San Felipe

Galveston

Refugio

Mexico

Matamoros

Houston Makes a Trade

Many of the Texans wanted to kill Santa Anna on the spot, but Houston had other ideas. The two men met under an oak tree, where Houston was nursing his wound, and began to negotiate. In the end, Santa Anna got his life and Houston got Texas. Less than a month later, before he was allowed to leave Texas, Santa Anna signed the Treaty of Velasco. Texas was to receive its independence, and the Mexican army was to move south of the Rio Grande.

Once Santa Anna reached Mexico, he claimed the treaty was invalid. He had a good case, since international law held that any agreement signed under pressure by a prisoner was not binding. In reality, however, the Mexicans lacked the strength to back up their claim. Santa Anna's defeat in Texas had left him politically weak, and he was soon occupied with revolts throughout Mexico.

Texas would remain an independent country for nine years. Sam Houston would twice be its president. On February 19, 1846, he presided at a ceremony at the log capital building in the new town of Austin. He lowered the Lone Star flag and held it to his chest as the Stars and Stripes was raised. The Republic of Texas, christened in the blood of the men of the Alamo, had become the state of Texas.

The Debate

More than 180 men died defending the Alamo. In so doing, they made themselves heroes in the eyes of Texans both then and now. They have been glorified by Hollywood; cities, counties, and schools by the hundreds are named for them. And yet, the key question has been debated ever since: Was the Battle of the Alamo worth the lives it cost? As T. R. Fehrenbach points out, "Gallantry of itself in battle is worthless, until its results may be assessed."[93]

Santa Anna himself claimed in later years, as have many others, that he could not have simply bypassed the Alamo, thus leaving a strong enemy force to his rear. This is simply untrue. Mexican forces at San Antonio eventually numbered about five thousand. Even as early as February 25, a small part of the Mexican army could have kept Travis penned up in the Alamo while the rest pushed on. Santa Anna's objective should have been to descend quickly on the more heavily populated Texian areas in the east, but his ego prevented him from doing so. He wanted a great personal triumph. "In our opinion all that bloodshed . . . was useless," wrote General Filisola, "having as its only objective an inconsiderate, childish and culpable [blamable] vanity."[94]

The Battle of the Alamo earned the rest of Texas twelve days. Militarily, the Tex-ans didn't accomplish much in that span; politically, they did. If Santa Anna had swept east, the convention at Washington-on-the-Brazos would never have met and never have declared independence, thus letting the Texans know precisely for what they were fighting.

The battle did help the Texas army in some respects. For one thing, Houston was away negotiating with the Cherokee in February. A rapid Mexican advance would have found the Texans without their best commander. Also, Travis's appeals did have some effect. When Houston finally arrived at Gonzales on March 11, more than a hundred volunteers awaited him—the core of the army that was to win at San Jacinto.

A Wounded Army

The military effect of the battle was felt much more by the Mexicans. Santa Anna's casualties damaged his army. To be sure, his battalions were brought back to full strength, but with raw recruits, not the seasoned troops he had specifically ordered for the assault. The Mexican dead, whether sixteen hundred or six hundred, represented, as Ruiz wrote, "the flower of the army."[95] One Mexican officer said af-

Long after the battle, the Alamo remains a symbol of the fight for Texas independence.

ter the battle, "It can truly be said that with another such victory as this we'll go to the devil."[96]

Even more important than the time or the lives it cost Santa Anna to conquer the Alamo was the way in which he did it. His cruelty there and at Goliad had a profound effect, not only in Texas, but also in the United States. American reaction to the rebellion had been mixed. Many in the north were against acquiring Texas, fearing it would enter as a state where slavery was legal, thus giving the South a political advantage. A Memphis, Tennessee, newspaper said, "We have been opposed to the Texan war from first to last, but our feelings we cannot suppress—some of our own bosom friends have fallen in the Alamo. We would avenge their death and spill the last drop of our blood upon the altar of Liberty."[97] Volunteer companies organized and began heading for Texas. Money was raised to help the Texans, from $100,000 in New York City to $516 raised by women in Bardstown, Kentucky, by selling quilts and pies.

In Texas, where it mattered most, Santa Anna's determination to kill all "foreign pirates" had a different effect. The Texans knew they must win or die. The Alamo and Goliad had shown them that they could expect no mercy if they were defeated. Just as important, this fear of death was combined with a burning anger. The Texans who retreated with Houston could have turned tail and run for the United States, but they were eager for a fight. Their attitude may have been what convinced Houston to turn toward San Jacinto and victory.

And so, although they delayed Santa Anna and inflicted serious damage to his army, the men who defended the Alamo may have achieved their greatest importance as symbols. Their courage, determination, and—finally—their deaths motivated others to win liberty or, like them, die trying. The ghosts of the vanquished—Travis, Bowie, Crockett, Dickinson, Bonham, Esparza, and all the rest—helped bring about eventual victory by ensuring that their fellow Texans did, indeed, remember the Alamo.

Notes

Introduction: Viewpoints

1. T. R. Fehrenbach, *Lone Star: A History of Texas and the Texans*. New York: Collier Books, 1968.

Chapter 1: The Mission

2. Quoted in Fehrenbach, *Lone Star*.
3. Quoted in Fehrenbach, *Lone Star*.
4. Quoted in Fehrenbach, *Lone Star*.
5. Quoted in Fehrenbach, *Lone Star*.
6. Quoted in Fehrenbach, *Lone Star*.

Chapter 2: The Rebellion

7. Quoted in Fehrenbach, *Lone Star*.
8. Quoted in Jeff Long, *Duel of Eagles: The Mexican and U.S. Fight for the Alamo*. New York: William Morrow, 1990.
9. Quoted in Albert A. Nofi, *The Alamo and the Texas War for Independence*. New York: Da Capo Press, 1994.
10. Quoted in Long, *Duel of Eagles*.
11. Quoted in Nofi, *The Alamo and the Texas War for Independence*.
12. Quoted in Fehrenbach, *Lone Star*.
13. Quoted in Albert A. Nofi, *The Alamo and the Texas War for Independence*.
14. Quoted in Wallace O. Chariton, *100 Days in Texas: The Alamo Letters*. Plano, TX: Wordware Publishing, 1990.
15. Quoted in Chariton, *100 Days in Texas*.
16. Quoted in Long, *Duel of Eagles*.
17. Quoted in Chariton, *100 Days in Texas*.
18. Quoted in John Myers Myers, *The Alamo*. Lincoln: University of Nebraska Press, 1948.
19. Quoted in Long, *Duel of Eagles*.
20. Quoted in Lon Tinkle, *13 Days to Glory*. New York: McGraw-Hill, 1958.

Chapter 3: The Siege: First Week

21. Quoted in Walter Lord, *A Time to Stand*. Lincoln: University of Nebraska Press, 1961.
22. Quoted in Lord, *A Time to Stand*.
23. Quoted in Tinkle, *13 Days to Glory*.
24. Quoted in Long, *Duel of Eagles*.
25. Quoted in Myers, *The Alamo*.
26. Quoted in Lord, *A Time to Stand*.
27. Quoted in Long, *Duel of Eagles*.
28. Quoted in Chariton, *100 Days in Texas*.
29. Quoted in H. Bailey Carroll et al., *Heroes of Texas*. Waco, TX: Texian Press, 1966.
30. Quoted in Bob Boyd, *The Texas Revolution: A Day-by-Day Account*. San Angelo, TX: San Angelo Standard-Times, 1986.

Chapter 4: The Siege: Second Week

31. Quoted in Nofi, *The Alamo and the Texas War for Independence*.
32. Quoted in Lord, *A Time to Stand*.
33. Quoted in Chariton, *100 Days in Texas*.
34. Quoted in Chariton, *100 Days in Texas*.
35. Quoted in Chariton, *100 Days in Texas*.
36. Quoted in Long, *Duel of Eagles*.
37. Quoted in Long, *Duel of Eagles*.
38. Quoted in Long, *Duel of Eagles*.
39. Quoted in Chariton, *100 Days in Texas*.
40. Quoted in Tinkle, *13 Days to Glory*.
41. Quoted in Tinkle, *13 Days to Glory*.
42. Quoted in Lord, *A Time to Stand*.
43. José Enrique de la Peña, *With Santa Anna in Texas*. Trans. and ed. Carmen Perry. College Station: Texas A&M University Press, 1975.
44. Quoted in Fehrenbach, *Lone Star*.
45. Quoted in Lord, *A Time to Stand*.
46. De la Peña, *With Santa Anna in Texas*.
47. Quoted in Chariton, *100 Days in Texas*.

48. Quoted in Lord, *A Time to Stand.*
49. Quoted in Tinkle, *13 Days to Glory.*

Chapter 5: The Assault

50. De la Peña, *With Santa Anna in Texas.*
51. De la Peña, *With Santa Anna in Texas.*
52. Quoted in Lord, *A Time to Stand.*
53. De la Peña, *With Santa Anna in Texas.*
54. De la Peña, *With Santa Anna in Texas.*
55. De la Peña, *With Santa Anna in Texas.*
56. De la Peña, *With Santa Anna in Texas.*
57. De la Peña, *With Santa Anna in Texas.*
58. Quoted in Nofi, *The Alamo and the Texas War for Independence.*
59. Quoted in Nofi, *The Alamo and the Texas War for Independence.*
60. Quoted in Long, *Duel of Eagles.*
61. Quoted in Myers, *The Alamo.*
62. Quoted in Long, *Duel of Eagles.*
63. De la Peña, *With Santa Anna in Texas.*
64. Quoted in Long, *Duel of Eagles.*
65. Quoted in Carroll, *Heroes of Texas.*
66. Quoted in Long, *Duel of Eagles.*
67. De la Peña, *With Santa Anna in Texas.*
68. Quoted in Long, *Duel of Eagles.*
69. Quoted in Lord, *A Time to Stand.*
70. De la Peña, *With Santa Anna in Texas.*
71. Quoted in Long, *Duel of Eagles.*
72. De la Peña, *With Santa Anna in Texas.*
73. Quoted in Lord, *A Time to Stand.*

Chapter 6: The Aftermath

74. Quoted in Chariton, *100 Days in Texas.*
75. Quoted in Long, *Duel of Eagles.*

76. Quoted in Nofi, *The Alamo and the Texas War for Independence.*
77. Quoted in Nofi, *The Alamo and the Texas War for Independence.*
78. Quoted in Long, *Duel of Eagles.*
79. Quoted in Long, *Duel of Eagles.*
80. Quoted in Long, *Duel of Eagles.*
81. Quoted in Long, *Duel of Eagles.*
82. Quoted in Long, *Duel of Eagles.*
83. Quoted in Long, *Duel of Eagles.*
84. De la Peña, *With Santa Anna in Texas.*
85. Quoted in Chariton, *100 Days in Texas.*
86. Quoted in Chariton, *100 Days in Texas.*
87. Quoted in Fehrenbach, *Lone Star.*
88. Quoted in Long, *Duel of Eagles.*
89. Quoted in Seymour V. Connor et al., *Battles of Texas.* Waco, TX: Texian Press, 1967.
90. Quoted in Fehrenbach, *Lone Star.*
91. Quoted in Connor, *Battles of Texas.*
92. Quoted in Nofi, *The Alamo and the Texas War for Independence.*

Epilogue: The Debate

93. Fehrenbach, *Lone Star.*
94. Quoted in Long, *Duel of Eagles.*
95. Quoted in Myers, *The Alamo.*
96. Quoted in Tinkle, *13 Days to Glory.*
97. Quoted in Long, *Duel of Eagles.*

For Further Reading

Alden Carter, *Last Stand at the Alamo*. New York: Franklin Watts, 1990. Short and easily read account of the Battle of the Alamo. Lavishly illustrated with maps, diagrams, full-color paintings, and photographs.

Fairfax Downey, *Texas and the War with Mexico*. New York: American Heritage Publishing Company, 1961. Excellent, wonderfully illustrated history of Spanish North America, starting with the explorers and continuing throughout the Mexican-American War that brought what would become Arizona, Utah, Nevada, and California into the United States.

Leonard Everett Fisher, *The Alamo*. New York: Holiday House, 1987. Well-told story of the Alamo from its founding as a mission to modern times. Good illustrations and excellent photographs, including many showing the evolution of the Alamo over the last one hundred years.

Nancy Haston Foster, *The Alamo and Other Texas Missions to Remember*. Houston, TX: Gulf Publishing Company, 1984. Provides not only history and photographs of most of the Texas missions, but also describes what visitors may still see there.

Jean Fritz, *Make Way for Sam Houston*. New York: G. P. Putnam's Sons, 1986. Excellent biography of the military leader and statesman. One of the few juvenile biographies that gives a great deal of attention to Houston's career after the Battle of San Jacinto.

Carol Hoff, *Johnny Texas*. Austin, TX: Jenkins Publishing Company, 1977. Ten-year-old Johann, an immigrant from Germany, gets caught up in the Texas Revolution. Reprint of the 1950 classic, one of the best pieces of juvenile fiction on Texas.

———, *Johnny Texas on the San Antonio Road*. Dallas: Hendrick-Long Publishing Company, 1984. Reprint of the 1953 sequel to *Johnny Texas*. Not quite as exciting as the first story, but still a good picture of life in the Republic of Texas.

John Jakes, *Susannah of the Alamo*. San Diego: Harcourt Brace Jovanovich, 1986. Highly fictionalized but very readable account of Susannah Dickinson's experiences at the Battle of the Alamo and shortly afterward. Ignores her sad later life.

Henry David Pope, *A Lady and a Lone Star Flag*. Bryan, TX: Brazos Valley Printing, 1986. Reprinting of a 1936 book telling the true story of Johanna Troutman, a Georgia woman who made the flag that flew over Goliad during the Texas Revolution.

J. A. Rickard, *Brief Biographies of Brave Texans*. Dallas: Hendrick-Long Publishing Company, 1980. Very good in that it goes beyond the usual roll call of Texas heroes to take in such people as Lorenzo de Zavala and Gail Borden, the inventor of condensed milk.

Dorothy Tutt Sinclair, *Tales of the Texians.* Bellaire, TX: Dorothy Sinclair Enterprises, 1985. Privately published by the author, this collection of short chapters tells the story of Texas from the Indians, through the Spanish mission days, to statehood.

Robert Penn Warren, *Remember the Alamo!* New York: Random House, 1958. One of the best histories of the Battle of the Alamo as written by one of America's finest authors. Highly accurate and vividly told.

Works Consulted

Kent Biffle, "Researcher Challenges Alamo Story," *Dallas Morning News*, July 16, 1995. Newspaper article about the research of Thomas Lindley that indicates errors in the traditional list of the men killed at the Alamo.

Bob Boyd, *The Texas Revolution: A Day-by-Day Account*. San Angelo, TX: San Angelo Standard-Times, 1986. Events during the Texas Revolution are recounted as if they were stories in a newspaper. Interesting reading, and the character sketches included at the back are very helpful.

H. Bailey Carroll et al., *Heroes of Texas*. Waco, TX: Texian Press, 1966. A collection of brief biographical sketches of most of the principal figures of the Texas Revolution, each accompanied by a color portrait.

Wallace O. Chariton, *100 Days in Texas: The Alamo Letters*. Plano, TX: Wordware Publishing, 1990. The story of the Texas Revolution, from shortly before the Battle of San Antonio to shortly before the Battle of San Jacinto, is told through excerpts of letters, proclamations, resolutions, and diaries of those involved.

Seymour V. Connor et al., *Battles of Texas*. Waco, TX: Texian Press, 1967. Brief accounts of Texas battles, not only those of the revolution, but also major Indian battles and the lone Civil War battle fought in Texas.

T. R. Fehrenbach, *Lone Star: A History of Texas and the Texans*. New York: Collier Books, 1968. This massive history of Texas from beginning to present day was the basis for the Public Broadcasting System's series of the same name. Not much detail on the battles of the revolution, but the chapters dealing with the Indians, Spanish, and French are excellent.

Joe B. Frantz, *Texas: A Bicentennial History*. New York: W. W. Norton, 1976. Vividly written, but Frantz had difficulty compressing all the information into the length (about two hundred pages) he was allowed.

Mary Ann Noonan Guerra, *The Alamo*. San Antonio, TX: The Alamo Press, 1983. Slim paperback book on the Alamo provides good information, not only about the battle, but also about the history of the mission and its fate since 1836.

C. D. Huneycutt, *The Alamo: An In-Depth Study of the Battle*. Privately published by the author, 1986. Highly opinionated version of the battle. The author is outspoken in condemning anyone who suggests that traditional views are incorrect. Good account of military strategy and fortifications.

Jeff Long, *Duel of Eagles: The Mexican and U.S. Fight for the Alamo*. New York: William Morrow, 1990. The small details woven throughout the story make this one of the most readable books on the subject. The author seems determined, however, to cast everyone in as bad a light as possible.

Walter Lord, *A Time to Stand*. Lincoln: University of Nebraska Press, 1961. One of the best nonscholarly works written about the Alamo. Grabs and holds the reader's attention. Good illustrations, bibliography, and index, but footnotes would have helped.

John Myers Myers, *The Alamo*. Lincoln: University of Nebraska Press, 1948. Section dealing with the history of the Alamo is one of the best to be found. Story of the battle is too often interrupted by long background sketches on major figures. Lack of index is a handicap.

Albert A. Nofi, *The Alamo and the Texas War for Independence*. New York: Da Capo Press, 1994. Paperback edition of the book originally published in 1982. Particularly useful in detailing Mexican troop movements. Small, interspersed vignettes provide excellent information without interrupting the narrative.

José Enrique de la Peña, *With Santa Anna in Texas*. Trans. and ed. by Carmen Perry. College Station: Texas A&M University Press, 1975. Fascinating account of the war from the standpoint of a Mexican officer. Gives particularly good picture of Santa Anna as a commander.

Lon Tinkle, *13 Days to Glory*. New York: McGraw-Hill, 1958. Exciting day-by-day account of the Battle of the Alamo. Not very scholarly, but one of the most popular books on the subject.

Index

Picture Credits

Cover photo: Corbis-Bettmann

Archive Photos, 11, 14

Archives & Information Services Division—Texas State Library, 42, 44, 47, 55, 68, 70

© Bernard Boutrit/Woodfin Camp & Associates, Inc., 43

Corbis-Bettmann, 49, 63, 67, 78

Culver Pictures, Inc., 17, 41, 52, 69

The Daughters of the Republic of Texas Library, 16, 22, 24 (sketch by Wiley Martin, CN96.367), 30 (*El Alamo* by Theodore Gentilz, gift of the Yanaguana Society), 39, 56 (CN96.38), 66 (gift of Eleanor Bomar, CN95.255), 75

Bella Hollingworth, 59

The Institute of Texan Cultures, 19

Library of Congress, 21, 26, 33, 35, 54, 58, 80

North Wind Picture Archives, 62

Stock Montage, Inc., 13, 27, 28, 50, 64, 83

Texas State Library, Austin, 36

About the Author

William W. Lace is a native of Fort Worth, Texas. He holds a bachelor's degree from Texas Christian University, a master's degree from East Texas State University, and a doctorate from the University of North Texas. After writing for newspapers in Baytown, Texas, and Fort Worth, he joined the University of Texas at Arlington, eventually becoming director of the News Service. He is now vice chancellor for public affairs at Tarrant County Junior College in Fort Worth. He and his wife Laura live in Arlington and have two grown children. Lace's other books include biographies of baseball player Nolan Ryan, artist Michelangelo, and statesman Winston Churchill, and histories of the Hundred Years' War and Elizabethan England.

DATE DUE

j	Lace, W.
F	The Alamo
390	
L18	
1998	

DISCARDED

02/98